A Celebration of
PRAIRIE BIRDS

A Celebration of
PRAIRIE BIRDS

Text & Photographs by
Wayne Lynch

Assisted by
Aubrey Lang

FIFTH
HOUSE

Published in Canada by Fifth House Publishers, 195 Allstate Parkway, Markham, Ontario, L3R 4T8

Published in the United States by Fifth House Publishers, 311 Washington Street, Brighton, Massachusetts 02135

www.fifthhousepublishers.ca

Fifth House Publishers acknowledges with thanks the Canada Council for the Arts and the Ontario Arts Council for their support of our publishing program. We acknowledge the financial support of the Government of Canada through the Canada Book Fund (CFB) for our publishing activities.

Library and Archives Canada Cataloguing in Publication
Title: Celebrating prairie birds / Wayne Lynch.
Other titles: Wild birds across the prairies
Names: Lynch, Wayne, author, photographer.
Description: Originally published as Wild birds across the prairies by Fifth House Publishers, Calgary, 1999. | Includes bibliographical references and index.
Identifiers: Canadiana 20200307207 | ISBN 9781927083574 (softcover)
Subjects: LCSH: Birds—Prairie Provinces. | LCSH: Birds—Prairie Provinces—Pictorial works.
Classification: LCC QL685.5.P7 L96 2020 | DDC 598.09712—dc23

Publisher Cataloging-in-Publication Data (US)
Names: Lynch, Wayne, author.
Title: Celebrating Prairie Birds / Wayne Lynch.
Description: Markham, Ontario : Fitzhenry and Whiteside, 2020. | Originally published by Fifth House, Calgary AB as Wild Birds Across the Prairies. | Summary: "The different wild habitats throughout the prairies combine to make the prairie grasslands, and the birds that fill its skies, a natural sanctuary to soothe the psyche, challenge the mind and rekindle the spirit. Grassland birds live complex and intriguing lives and in this book I share many fascinating details that makes the creatures so interesting and satisfying to watch"– Provided by publisher.
Identifiers: ISBN 978-1-92708-357-4 (paperback)
Subjects: LCSH: Grassland birds. | Grassland birds – Behavior. | BISAC: NATURE / Animals / Birds.
Classification: LCC QL698.3L963 | DDC [E] – dc23

Editor: Charlene Dobmeier
Text and cover design: Tanya Montini

Printed in Hong Kong by Sheck Wah Tong Printing

2 4 6 5 3 1

www.fifthhousepublishers.ca

For Myrna—
Whose uncommon generosity and warm hospitality
was my introduction to the prairies

For Lorne—
A much admired conservationist and
tireless advocate for prairie preservation

TABLE OF CONTENTS

‹ The sculpted sandstone badlands of Alberta's Milk River Valley were a sacred site for vision quests by Indigenous people.

The exposed bedrock of Horseshoe ❯
Canyon in southern Alberta dates back
to the time of the dinosaurs, more than
66 million years ago.

PREFACE & INTRODUCTION

It was a bitterly cold April morning. I had slept in the open under a crystalline prairie sky, and a rim of frost glittered on the sagebrush near my head. I could hear the familiar plop and gurgle of sage-grouse calling on their dancing grounds just 20 meters (65 ft.) away. Barely awake and reluctant to leave the warmth and comfort of my sleeping bag, I slowly crept on my hands and knees to my photo blind. It was 5:15 a.m. I shivered and waited in the dark. After an hour, the sun finally cracked the horizon, flooding the prairie with amber light and highlighting the feathered beauty of the two dozen magnificent sage-grouse that surrounded my blind. For the next two hours I watched them strut their stuff, fight, chase, and mate. Witnessing this wildlife spectacle was enough reward; it mattered little if I captured the moment with my camera. As has happened so often I was mesmerized by the natural wonder of birds.

I became enchanted by the prairie grasslands more than 40 years ago and have been bewitched by birds even longer. This book combines both of these personal passions. But it is more than a book about the birds of the prairies; it is a celebration

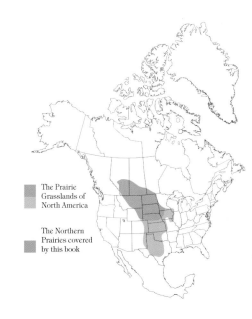

The Prairie Grasslands of North America

The Northern Prairies covered by this book

❮ The individual trees in a cluster of prairie aspens may be genetically identical and members of a clone that share a common root system sometimes thousands of years old.

of the beauty and biology of the natural world. Originally, native prairie grasslands occupied the entire central core of North America, roughly 138 million hectares (340 million ac.). This vast expanse of grass and sky stretched for over 2,000 kilometers (1,200 mi.) from the aspen parklands of western Canada south to Texas, and from the jagged summits of the Rocky Mountains to the eastern hardwood forests. Today, more than 80 percent of the continent's grasslands are no more than a memory, and native prairie continues to disappear at a rate of 40,000 hectares (100,000 ac.) a year—victims of urban sprawl and humanity's insatiable appetite for cropland. It is no surprise that grassland birds are declining more rapidly than any other avian community in North America. The best way to preserve these last remnants of prairie grasslands and their wildlife is to understand what we will lose if we do nothing to protect them. Grassland birds live complex and intriguing lives. In *A Celebration of Prairie Birds* I share with you the many fascinating details that make these creatures so interesting and satisfying to watch.

In 1999, I wrote *Wild Birds Across the Prairies*. The book was a tribute to the subtle beauty and fascinating biology of the birds that inhabit one of the most threatened large ecosystems on the planet. Over time, I moved on to other projects: northern bears, the Arctic, the Sonoran Desert, the Galapagos Islands, the boreal forest, penguins of the world, owls of North America, Florida manatees, the Everglades, and American alligators. In the intervening decades, I returned often to the prairies to refresh my soul with the fragrant scent of pasture sage and the hypnotic melodies of meadowlarks, pipits, and longspurs. Now, 20 years later, it is time to write again about the prairie birds I so love. Much of what was interesting and important in 1999 remains so today. Instead of writing a completely new book, I decided to make a good book better and build from *Wild Birds Across the Prairies*. I have updated and enriched the science in many of the species accounts, added some completely new ones, and rewritten others to reflect exciting new discoveries in biology. Photography has always been a vital component of every book I've written, and *A Celebration of Prairie Birds* features fresh new

〈 Golden bean is one of the earliest flowers to bloom in the prairie grasslands.

images that reflect the heightened light sensitivity and action-freezing attributes of modern digital photography as well as my continued fascination with the visual wonder of the prairies and its avian inhabitants.

Roughly 250 species of birds are found in the prairies of Canada and the northern United States. They can be divided into four convenient categories. The first group, which accounts for about 15 percent of the total, is the year-round residents, including such familiar birds as grouse and some owls. Seasonal breeders that move to the prairies for the spring and summer are the largest group; roughly half of all prairie birds fall into this category. A third group, the migrants, passes through the prairies in the spring and autumn en route to and from the boreal forest or the Arctic. This group consists mainly of shorebirds, waterfowl, and wood warblers and makes up about a quarter of the total bird population. The winter visitors are the smallest group, just 10 percent of all prairie birds, and includes such favorites as birds of prey, finches, and some Arctic owls. To provide as much diversity as possible, I have included birds from all four categories. I also selected birds that are relatively easy to find and those with which I have had considerable field experience. In addition, I included birds that have been studied well; research having revealed fascinating details of their biology.

Another way I tried to make the book more diverse was to choose birds from a variety of prairie habitats. The habitat that most people associate with the prairies is the rolling grassy plains. Yet the prairie grasslands is a wonderful and surprising mosaic of many habitats. It includes wetlands, such as sloughs and marshes rimmed with waving stands of cattails, as well as lazy, winding rivers, and large alkaline lakes. It also contains rolling dunescapes, sculpted badlands of multicolored sandstone, and inviting wooded river valleys and coulees where you can retreat from the light and glare of the open sky. Together, these different wild habitats combine to make the prairie grasslands, and the birds that fill its skies, a natural sanctuary to soothe the psyche, challenge the mind, and rekindle the spirit.

Cattails like to have "wet feet" during ❯
the growing season and occupy the
edge of many prairie sloughs.

SPECIES ACCOUNTS

RED-NECKED GREBE *Podiceps grisegena*

Family Details

Grebe Family (Podicipedidae), 22 species worldwide, 6 prairie species

Grebes are a common group of waterbirds found on sloughs and lakes across the prairies. Although they resemble ducks in size, they have a slender pointed bill, not a flat one as do most ducks. Grebes are superb divers. The position of their legs at the back of their body gives them power and maneuverability in the water. Because their legs are so far to the rear, they walk with difficulty, and it is almost impossible for them to take off from land. Takeoff from the water, however, is not much better. All grebes have relatively small wings for their body size, so they must patter across the surface of the water for quite a distance before they gain enough speed to become airborne. When swimming, these attractive waterbirds have the uncanny ability to disappear underwater without a ripple, and the speed with which they do this has earned them several colorful nicknames: "devil-diver," "hell-diver," and "water witch."

Field Identification

The red-necked grebe has a stout yellow-and-black bill, a long chestnut-colored neck, white throat and cheeks, and a black forehead and cap. Male and female plumage is almost identical.

Where to Find

This grebe is usually found on lakes and larger sloughs with cattails or bulrushes bordering the shoreline.

Wintering Grounds

It spends the winter on salt water along the Atlantic and Pacific coasts of the continent.

Diet and Feeding Habits

The red-neck makes dives that last between 20 and 40 seconds. It feeds near the bottom on small fish, aquatic insects, tadpoles, and tiger salamanders.

Breeding Biology

The red-necked grebe, in common with the other family members, is a loudmouth lover. Courting pairs swim side by side, their crests raised, and together they sing an entertaining duet that sounds like a loud horse whinny. Typically, a nesting pair defends a territory of about 4 hectares (10 ac.), so large lakes and sloughs may contain several pairs of these noisy birds. In May and June, they build a floating nest of aquatic vegetation, which they anchor to cattails or rushes in water about a meter (3 ft.) deep. A clutch of three to six blue-white eggs is incubated for about three weeks, with both sexes sharing in the nest duties. The downy chicks leave the nest soon after they hatch, and although they can swim right away they spend the first three weeks of life riding on their parents' backs.

‹ The red-necked grebe lands with a belly flop when it settles on the water.

The red-necked grebe, like most grebes, generally mates with a new partner every year.

(left) The red-necked grebe is one of the most vocal grebes. (upper right) It took several minutes for this grebe to swallow the tiger salamander. (lower right) The floating nest of a grebe makes it safe from most predators.

EARED GREBE *Podiceps nigricollis*

Family Details

Grebe Family (Podicipedidae), 22 species worldwide, 6 prairie species *See Red-necked Grebe for a general discussion of the Grebe Family.*

Field Identification

The eared grebe has bright red eyes; a slightly upturned, thin, black bill; rusty sides; and a black head and neck adorned with a pair of distinctive golden "ear" tufts. The female's coloration, especially her golden ear tufts, is slightly duller than the male's.

Where to Find

Eared grebes are gregarious in all seasons and they prefer larger sloughs and lakes with enough open water to support multiple pairs of breeding birds.

Wintering Grounds

They sometimes winter inland in Nevada, New Mexico, and Utah but are more common along the Pacific and Atlantic coasts of North America.

(top) The courtship displays of the eared ❯ grebe often include the "penguin" dance. *(bottom)* Newly hatched grebelets are ferried and fed by both parents.

Diet and Feeding Habits

The bird feeds on leeches, dragonfly larvae, diving beetles, mollusks, small fish, and amphibians. Lobed toes, characteristic of all grebes, enable the bird to propel itself to depths of 7 meters (23 ft.), although it more commonly forages in shallow water.

Breeding Biology

The eared grebe frequently breeds in large colonies, sometimes containing several thousand pairs. The nest is a mound of green and rotting vegetation floating in water as shallow as 10 centimeters (4 in.). I have flooded my chest waders often enough pursuing photographs of these handsome grebes to know they frequently nest in much deeper water. Many years ago, I photographed a dense colony of eared grebes in Wascana Park in the center of Regina, Saskatchewan. Most of the nests were 3 or 4 meters (10 or 13 ft.) apart, but in a few cases they were almost touching one another.

Eared grebes lay three to five chalky, bluish white eggs that soon become stained brown. Whenever a parent leaves the eggs, it covers them with rotting nesting material to hide them from the sharp eyes of predators, such as crows and gulls. Thus the pale eggs quickly turn brown. In *The Birds of Alberta*, Ray and Jim Salt mused: "It is surprising that anything could hatch in such a sodden mess, but after about three weeks, grey and white fluffy youngsters, all neck and legs, peer out from under the parent at the watery world around them." The chicks leave the nest within a day of hatching and immediately climb onto a parent's back where they can snuggle under a wing to shelter themselves from cold spring downpours, hail, and the heat of the sun. In mild weather, the small grebelets ride with just their heads poking out.

➔ Trivia Tidbit

Young grebes are the original skinheads, and they have a novel way of communicating with their parents. The boldly striped youngsters have a triangular patch of bare skin on the top of their head as well as one in front of each eye that swell and become flushed with red whenever the chicks get excited, especially when they are begging for food. Scientists speculate that the parents may use the color of the skin to monitor a chick's hunger.

A grebelet swallows a bloodworm, ❯
the aquatic larva of a midge.

HORNED GREBE *Podiceps auritus*

Family Details

Grebe Family (Podicipedidae), 22 species worldwide, 6 prairie species
See Red-necked Grebe for a general discussion of the Grebe Family.

Field Identification

This medium-sized grebe has bright crimson eyes, a straight black bill tipped with white, rusty sides and neck, and a black head with golden "horns." The female's plumage is slightly duller than the male's. The horned grebe can be easily confused with the eared grebe. The neck color of the two birds is the easiest way to distinguish between them.

Where to Find

The horned grebe tends to select sloughs of open water that are fairly small, often less than 1 hectare (2.5 ac.) in size.

Wintering Grounds

This small, handsome waterbird overwinters along the Atlantic and Pacific coasts of North America, within sight of the shore, and on freshwater wetlands in the southeastern United States.

Diet and Feeding Habits

Although it may feed on the surface, taking water striders, back swimmers, and mosquito larvae, more often it dives for its meals and hunts small fish, tadpoles, leeches, and other aquatic invertebrates. During these dives, the grebe may stay submerged for up to three minutes and travel over 150 meters (490 ft.) underwater. With such underwater endurance it's not surprising these birds sometimes seem to disappear.

Breeding Biology

The horned grebe is usually a solitary nester, but four or five pairs may form a loose colony on larger lakes and marshes. Courtship includes a "weed dance" in which the partners, each with a beak full of soggy weeds, rush side by side across the water's surface. Head-shaking and bill-touching displays complete the ceremony.

The nest consists of a water-logged platform of floating weeds usually surrounded by a few stems of cattails or bulrushes. Strong prairie winds can whip up sizeable waves on the surface of a slough, and without the protection of some kind of emergent vegetation a grebe nest would soon be swamped. The pair never retrieves eggs that get washed out of a nest during a storm. The four to five nest-stained eggs hatch after 24 days. For the first month or so, the chicks eat, sleep, and travel on a parent's back. As they get older, they paddle behind the weary adults incessantly begging to be fed, as many avian offspring seem to do. The free lunches stop when the young grebes are about two months old and have begun to fly.

→ Trivia Tidbit

The waterproof plumage on a grebe is especially soft and thick, and it may have over 20,000 feathers on its body. In the late 1800s, grebes were heavily hunted, and their thick feathers were marketed as "grebe fur" and used to adorn the capes and hats of stylish women of the era. Long before the grebe furriers came along, however, the grebes were using their own feathers in a way unique among birds. Grebes regularly swallow feathers that loosen during preening. Over half the contents of a horned grebe's stomach may consist of feathers. Researchers speculate that the feathers may line the grebe's stomach and protect it from sharp fish bones. Another possibility is that the feathers may filter sharp food debris and prevent it from entering the intestine. The wad of feathers, bones, and debris is then regurgitated and spit out as a harmless pellet. Regurgitating a pellet every other day may also minimize the buildup of stomach parasites, which can represent a considerable health hazard. No matter why grebes feast on feathers, the behavior is crucial to them. Day-old grebe chicks are fed small feathers by their parents, sometimes even before they are given any food!

The male horned grebe often brings a ›
gift of nesting material prior to mating
and then ends the brief mounting with
a penguin display in which it vigorously
treads water and rises upright.

PIED-BILLED GREBE *Podilymbus podiceps*

Family Details

Grebe Family (Podicipedidae), 22 species worldwide, 6 prairie species. *See Red-necked Grebe for a general discussion of the Grebe Family.*

Field Identification

The pied-billed grebe is the smallest and most secretive of the prairie grebes. On its summer breeding grounds, the surest way to identify this small grebe is by its beak. The bird has a bluish white, hen-like beak with a black band around it. Notwithstanding its all-brown coloration and black throat, the pied-billed grebe is anything but plain looking.

Where to Find

The pied-bill likes dense stands of cattails and bulrushes and frequently settles on sloughs and small ponds that have relatively little open water, sometimes with as little as 20 percent. In this way, it differs from other prairie grebes, which prefer less vegetation and more open water.

Wintering Grounds

The pied-bill migrates in small numbers at night, as do all grebes, and most have left the prairies by the end of October. The majority migrate to inland lakes and marshes in the southern United States, although some overwinter on salt water along the southern coast of the country.

Diet and Feeding Habits

One spring, I watched an ambitious pied-bill try to swallow a large leopard frog. The bird repeatedly shook the frog, dropped it in the water, and picked it up again. After several minutes of such "tenderizing," the bird was still unable to dismember or swallow its catch. The grebe swam behind some cattails before I saw how the meal ended. Pied-billed grebes normally tackle much smaller prey than frogs. They hunt in shallow water for small fish; aquatic beetles; bugs; leeches; and the larvae of midges, dragonflies, and damselflies. When hunting, they usually stay submerged for less than 15 seconds, although dives can last up to four times that long and cover distances of 12 meters (39 ft.).

The soggy nest of a pied-billed grebe. ❯

Breeding Biology

The pied-bill is heard far more often than it is seen. The male's territorial song is a loud, throaty *kow, kow, kow,* which can be heard up to a kilometer (0.6 mi.) away. The loud call penetrates the thick stands of cattails and rushes in which these birds live, and not surprisingly their courtship consists mainly of vocal displays. The elaborate visual displays used by the other prairie grebes in open water would be much less effective in the confusion of stems and leaves where pied-bills prefer to live.

Pairs build a soggy platform nest of vegetation in shallow water. I have often searched for their nests and can attest to how well hidden they are among the cattails. In many cases, the birds will build two nests but use only the second one to cradle their eggs. The first nest is used for loafing and copulation. Pied-bills lay four to seven plain, whitish eggs and both partners share in the three-week incubation. The adults care for the newly hatched chicks for roughly a week or two, by which time the young grebes are hunting for themselves and making their first clumsy flights.

A wary pied-bill can sink from ❯
sight with barely a ripple.

AMERICAN WHITE PELICAN

Pelecanus erythrorhynchos

Family Details

Pelican Family (Pelecanidae), 8 species worldwide, 1 prairie species

The pelican is hard to confuse with any other waterbird. They are massive birds with a wingspan reaching nearly 3 meters (10 ft.); some individuals may weigh as much as 13.5 kilograms (30 lb.), making them among the heaviest of flying birds. Their distinctive large beak and pouch inspired the famous limerick by Dixon Lanier Merritt: "A marvellous bird is the pelican, his bill holds more than his belly can. He can hold in his beak, enough food for a week, and I wonder how the hell he can." A pelican's beak, in fact, can hold nearly 11 liters (3 gal.) of water—a hundred times the capacity of the human mouth.

Field Identification

The pelican is a large white bird with black wingtips visible only when the bird is in flight. The black on the wing is the surest way to distinguish the white pelican from the tundra swan, another large white bird seen in the prairies. Early in the breeding season, both male and female white pelicans have a horny fin on the top of their upper beak that drops off soon after egg laying is finished.

‹ The pelican has the largest average wingspan of any prairie bird. This allows it to soar on thermals and conserve energy.

Despite its large size, the pelican is a graceful flier, and groups of them may soar high on the updrafts of warm midday thermals.

Where to Find

The white pelican prefers large lakes with secluded islands for nesting. The birds may use smaller lakes and sloughs for fishing and loafing.

Wintering Grounds

The pelican winters in central California and along the Pacific coast as far south as Guatemala, and also along the shores of the Gulf of Mexico. It returns to the prairies in early May.

Diet and Feeding Habits

The white pelican eats fish, mostly species ignored by human anglers, and catches them in shallow water, 0.3 to 2.5 meters (1 to 8 ft.) deep. They commonly fish in the open areas of sloughs and marshes, along lakeshores, and below rapids. They locate fish by sight during the day and by touch during the night. The white pelican frequently hunts in groups, a line of swimming

birds driving the fish ahead of them. Over and over again (four to six times per minute) each bird dips its bill and scoops up a pouch full of water. The dipping tends to become more coordinated when they find fish. A pelican trying to swallow a large fish may be attacked by another pelican wanting to steal its meal. An adult bird consumes about 1.5 kilograms (3 lb.) of fish a day. The white pelican, unlike its relative the brown pelican, never dives for fish from the air.

Breeding Biology

The pelican nests in large colonies, containing up to several hundred pairs, on secluded islands free from predators, such as red foxes and coyotes. Nesting colonies are extremely vulnerable to human disturbance, and a single visit early in the nesting season may cause an entire colony to desert.

Courtship includes "circle-flying" in which one or more pairs circle and soar above a nesting lake. The nest is a simple shallow depression on the ground sparsely lined with rocks, sticks, and rushes. In large colonies, the nests are usually spaced close together, typically just beyond the pecking distance of irritable neighbors. Beginning in June, two large, dull white eggs are incubated in shifts by both parents. After about 30 days, a pair of orange, naked, wrinkled, wobbly necked "space aliens" crack their way into the world. The first chick usually hatches a day or two before its sibling and grows much faster. The second chick rarely survives, usually dying from starvation and continual pecking by its nestmate.

At around two and a half weeks the adults begin to leave their chicks unattended and the youngsters gather in pods, or crèches. Crèching may offer some protection from aerial predators, such as large gulls, ravens, bald eagles, and great horned owls. Parents recognize the distinctive "whining grunt" of their chick and feed only their own. Colonies are abandoned in late August and early September.

→ **Trivia Tidbit**

Fifty years ago, fewer than 16,000 breeding pairs of American white pelicans were left in the birds' nesting range in central North America. Today, there are more than 120,000 breeding birds and their population continues to increase at 5 percent per year.

⟨ Pelicans commonly roost in shallow water ⟩ in groups at night. The groups disperse to feeding areas shortly after sunrise.

DOUBLE-CRESTED CORMORANT

Phalacrocorax auritus

Family Details

Cormorant Family (Phalacrocoracidae), 38 to 42 species world-wide, 1 prairie species

The cormorants are a group of medium-sized diving birds with long slim necks and slender hooked beaks. On land, the birds often perch with their wings outstretched. They rest like this to dry their feathers, which become waterlogged after a short time of swimming. The bird's soggy plumage probably makes them less buoyant, and as a result they are able to dive more easily. Most people associate cormorants with the seaside, and they may seem out of place in the arid prairies. However, the prairie-nesting, double-crested cormorant is extremely adaptable and ranges throughout central North America as well as in the Caribbean, in the coastal areas of the Gulf of Mexico, and on the Pacific coast from Alaska to the Baja Peninsula in Mexico.

Field Identification

The cormorant is a large black bird with a long neck and tail and a featherless, bright orange throat patch. In flight, the bird's neck is outstretched, unlike a heron, which hunches its head between its shoulders. When traveling in groups, cormorants fly silently in V-formation or in a line. The bird's most photogenic feature is its bright green eyes, which match the beauty of the finest polished jade.

Where to Find

The cormorant prefers large rivers, sloughs, and lakes.

Wintering Grounds

It spends the cold winter months on coastal and inland waterways in the southeastern and southwestern United States.

Diet and Feeding Habits

The cormorant is an agile diving bird that feeds mainly on fish but also eats crayfish, frogs, and salamanders. Cormorants, like grebes and loons, are foot-propelled divers that swim with powerful strokes of their large webbed feet. Among prairie birds, cormorants are the deepest divers, reaching depths of 25 meters (82 ft.), although they usually hunt in much shallower water. When a cormorant catches a fish it brings it to the surface before swallowing it. This habit sometimes gets the bird into trouble. When they can, pelicans attack cormorants and steal their fish. I once saw a bald eagle swoop down on a fishing cormorant. The startled cormorant dropped its catch and in the flash of a talon, the eagle flew off with the meal.

Breeding Biology

Their typically crowded colonies can be found on secluded islands in the middle of large sloughs and lakes. Less commonly, they also nest in the tops of dead trees. I have watched one ground-nesting colony in southeastern Alberta for several decades. Fifty to 60 pairs nest on an island about 0.5 kilometers (0.3 mi.) from the shoreline. By late May in a typical year, the bulky nests of cattails, rushes, and sticks have been built, the eggs (three to four per nest) have been laid, and the first of the rubber-necked youngsters has hatched. Nothing is homelier than a wrinkled, featherless, black cormorant chick, and its lack of good looks is not the only strike against it. Cormorants lay their eggs at two- to three-day intervals, and the parents begin to incubate as soon as the first egg is laid. As a result, the first chick may be more than a week old when the last chick finally cracks loose. When fish are plentiful everyone in the family is fed, but when the meals are meager the smallest chicks starve. Sometimes only one chick out of four may survive. Biologists call this behavior "facultative brood reduction." This simply means a cormorant pair starts out with the largest family it can possibly feed and the prevailing food conditions determine how many chicks survive.

→ Trivia Tidbit

The cormorant and the pelican incubate their eggs differently from all other prairie birds. Most birds have a small, featherless, vascularized area of skin on their belly called a "brood patch," which they use to warm their eggs. Cormorants and pelicans have no brood patch. Instead they use the large webs on their feet to cover their eggs and warm them. Breakage in cormorant eggs is rare, as they have especially thick shells.

‹ The eye muscles of the double-crested ›
   cormorant are especially strong allowing
   it to see well in air and underwater.

AMERICAN BITTERN *Botaurus lentiginosus*

Family Details

Heron Family (Ardeidae), 62 species worldwide, 3 prairie species

The family includes the herons, egrets, and bitterns, a familiar group of medium-sized to large wading birds. All of them have long legs, a long flexible neck, and a lengthy pointed bill used to grab frogs, fish, crustaceans, and aquatic insects.

During the breeding season, in many species, both the male and female have long delicate plumes adorning their head, neck, and body. A century ago, hundreds of thousands of herons and egrets were shamelessly slaughtered in North America for their feathers, which were used to embellish women's hair and trim their dresses and hats. In the 1880s, in the heyday of this fashion trend, egret feathers were worth five times their weight in gold! Many herons and egrets nest in large colonies, making their slaughter that much easier. Today, heron and egret numbers have recovered, and the birds are a common sight in the wetlands of the continent.

Field Identification

The American bittern is a chunky, medium-sized wading bird. The sexes are identical and are mottled brown on their head and back with brown and white vertical streaks on their underside. A black "moustache" line extends down the sides of their neck. When the shy bittern is alarmed, it faces toward the danger, points its beak skyward, and freezes. The vertical streaking on the bird's neck and chest blends in well with the cattails and bulrushes where it lives, and camouflages the bird. The trickster even sways slowly from side to side to imitate the movement of windblown reeds.

Where to Find

The bittern is widespread throughout the prairies, although it is secretive and hard to find. It prefers medium to large marshes with thick stands of tall cattails and bulrushes. It rarely leaves the protective cover of vegetation.

‹ The vertical streaks on a bittern's breast blend in with the vertical stalks of cattails where it hunts.

Wintering Grounds

The bittern needs year-round access to open water, and those from the prairies may overwinter from the southern edge of the United States through Mexico and Central America. Most migrate from the prairies in September or October and return again in early May.

Diet and Feeding Habits

The bittern is most active in the half light of dusk and dawn. The bird is a master of patience, waiting motionless for long periods to catch its prey. It hunts aquatic beetles and other insects, frogs, toads, salamanders, garter snakes, and even small mammals, such as meadow voles. Biologists believe that the vertical streaking on the underside of the bird, though effective camouflage against predators, evolved primarily to hide the bird from its prey and to help it hunt.

Breeding Biology

The eerie call of the male bittern is one of my favorite marsh sounds. Authors James Hancock and James Kushlan described the call in The Herons Handbook. "On the breeding ground the American bittern gives a loud booming or pumping sound. The boom of this species is invariably described as resembling the noise of an old-fashioned hand pump, or of hammering a stake into muddy ground, leading to two of the bird's nicknames— 'stake-driver' and 'thunder pumper'."

The reclusive nature of the bittern makes the bird difficult to observe and study, and many aspects of its biology are still unknown. A male "booms" for at least two reasons: to attract a female and to deter rivals. Bitterns nest in defended territories, sometimes within 40 meters (131 ft.) of a neighboring pair. Even though male bitterns are monogamous, they are still the avian version of the deadbeat dad. The female, alone, builds the family nest of reeds, rushes, and cattails; incubates the three to five eggs; and feeds and broods the young. Young bitterns leave their nest, which is on the ground and hidden in thick cattails, when they are one or two weeks old. After that, the female continues to feed them intermittently for another couple of weeks while the youngsters perfect their hunting skills.

‹ Two-week-old bittern chicks puff themselves up and hiss to intimidate a predator.

GREAT BLUE HERON *Ardea herodias*

Family Details

Heron Family (Ardeidae), 62 species worldwide, 3 prairie species

See North American Bittern for a general discussion of the Heron Family.

Field Identification

The great blue is the largest heron in North America and stands about 60 centimeters (24 in.) tall. The bird might better be called the great gray heron since most of its neck and body are medium gray. The heron also has a distinctive black stripe over its eyes. In flight, the great blue holds its neck retracted in an S-shape. The position of its neck is the best way to distinguish the heron from the sandhill crane, another large gray bird with which the heron is sometimes confused. The crane flies with its neck fully extended.

Where to Find

The great blue heron is widespread throughout the prairies and is commonly found along the banks of many rivers and streams and around the shorelines of lakes, large sloughs, and irrigation ponds.

❮ The great blue heron has specialized feathers on its breast that grow continuously and fray. The bird combs this "powder down" through its plumage to remove fish slime and other oily dirt.

Wintering Grounds

Most herons from the northern prairies overwinter on freshwater wetlands or coastal marshes and shorelines across the southern United States. The birds migrate south in September and October, and many return by the end of March.

Diet and Feeding Habits

The great blue eats mainly fish. It hunts either by slowly walking through the shallows or by standing still in water up to its belly, waiting for a fish to swim by. The heron, like most wading birds, is not a fussy feeder, and although it may have dietary preferences it will rarely pass up an easy meal. As a result, the great blue also eats aquatic insects, snails, frogs, salamanders, snakes, and any unwary mammal small enough for the bird to swallow whole, including an adult Richardson's ground squirrel. Herons have even been known to tackle muskrats. In one account, a heron battled with one of these chisel-toothed rodents for over an hour before the bird finally killed the muskrat and swallowed it in a single gulp.

Breeding Biology

The great blue heron, which may live for 20 years, pairs with a different partner every spring. When the herons return to the prairies in late March, they may form temporary flocks on "gathering grounds" where they likely choose a mate for the coming season. Courtship includes a number of elaborate displays: sky-pointing, bill-dueling, ceremonial preening, twig-shaking, and bill-clacking.

In the prairies, the great blue nests in small colonies of several dozen pairs or less. It usually builds a large nest of sticks, but often a pair may reuse an old nest from a previous season, adding new sticks to the pile. These refurbished nests can become quite bulky and may measure a meter (3 ft.) in diameter, a meter deep, and weigh up to 50 kilograms (110 lb.). Trees and islands are the most popular nesting sites in the prairies, since both offer the herons protection from predatory coyotes and red foxes.

The eggs of the great blue heron are a beautiful greenish blue, and a clutch of four eggs is the most common. Both parents share the four-week incubation, with the female usually taking the night shift. The eggs hatch roughly one to two days apart, so the growing chicks vary greatly in size. When food is scarce the smallest chick starves to death. The antics of wobbly necked young herons are comical to watch, and their appearance is just as amusing. The bug-eyed young chicks are covered with patchy clumps of gray down that is especially bushy on the top of the bird's head, giving it a punk appearance, as if it has just stuck its toes into a wall socket.

Both parents feed regurgitated globs of food to the chicks, and a pair may make dozens of feeding visits to the nest in a day. The gangly chicks are nearly two months old when they finally begin to fly, and they return to the nest to be fed for another three weeks after that.

BLACK-CROWNED NIGHT-HERON
Nycticorax nycticorax

Family Details

Heron Family (Ardeidae), 62 species worldwide, 3 prairie species
See North American Bittern for a general discussion of the Heron Family.

Field Identification

The night-heron is a medium-sized stocky heron, similar in size and build to the American bittern. Both have relatively short legs and a short neck, compared with the tall, stately great blue heron. Male and female adult night-herons are similar in appearance and have a black cap, black back, gray wings, and creamy underparts. At close range, the birds have attractive ruby-red eyes, which make them unmistakable. Young night-herons less than a year old are brown with white streaking overall and can be easily confused with an adult American bittern.

Where to Find

The black-crowned night-heron is the most widespread heron in the world and is found on every continent except Australia and Antarctica. In the prairies, this adaptable heron is locally common in large sloughs and marshes, but because of its nocturnal habits it is often overlooked. During the peak chick-feeding period the bird may be active during the day, but generally it spends the daylight hours hidden in thick cattails.

Wintering Grounds

Most night-herons leave the prairies by late September. Birds banded in Saskatchewan and Alberta have been recovered in freshwater marshes and mangrove swamps in Mexico, Texas, Florida, and Cuba.

Diet and Feeding Habits

Typically, the night-heron feeds from early evening to early morning. The bird's nocturnal habits reduce competition with the great blue heron and the bittern, which hunt more often in the daylight. The diet of the night-heron has been studied extensively, and, as you might predict, for a bird with such a cosmopolitan range it is an opportunistic omnivore. In an Alberta study, the herons ate stickleback fish, leopard frogs, chorus frogs, toads, dragonflies, diving beetles, blackbird nestlings, grasshoppers, crickets, water striders, and meadow voles. The night-heron hunts by slowly stalking the shallows or standing motionless, waiting patiently for prey to move within range of its lightning jab.

Breeding Biology

The black-crown is faithfully monogamous during the breeding season but mates with a different partner every year. The birds nest colonially, building platforms of twigs and weed stalks in the middle of dense stands of cattails and bulrushes. In the prairies, night-herons often nest close to noisy colonies of Franklin's gulls.

The aggressive gulls may provide the herons with protection by mobbing egg predators, such as crows, black-billed magpies, and ring-billed and California gulls. The black-crown repays the Franklins by eating their unattended chicks. No one ever said Nature was fair.

In Alberta, egg-laying begins in late April and early May, earlier than other prairie herons. The birds lay three to four greenish blue eggs, and the parents share the 23- to 26-day incubation period. Both adults also feed the young. The insatiable chicks grab the parents' beaks to stimulate them to regurgitate warm, gooey meals. As the chicks get larger, the parents simply dump food on the nest and the young gobble it up. Veteran heron researcher Dr. Bill Davis Jr. wrote, "Young chicks are quite aggressive, and often deposit their most recent meal on an investigator"—a polite way of saying they puke and peck. Night-heron nestlings fledge by the time they are six or seven weeks old, but they continue to beg for food from their parents and any other adult they encounter. At this age, most of the time they are unsuccessful.

‹ *(top)* The black-crown is one of the few birds to use tools. It is known to toss edible or inedible buoyant objects into the water hoping to lure a fish to within striking distance. *(bottom)* The juvenile night-heron is sometimes mistaken for an American bittern because both have streaky brown plumage.

‹ *(opposite)* An adult black-crown in breeding plumage has two or three long, thin white plumes draping from the back of its head.

WHITE-FACED IBIS *Plegadis chihi*

Family Details

Ibis and Spoonbill Family (Threskiornithidae), 32 species world-wide, 1 prairie species

Ibises are medium-sized wading birds with long legs; long necks; and a long, slender, down-curved bill. They use primarily touch rather than vision to locate their prey, and the tip of their bill is richly supplied with sensory cells for this purpose.

Ibises often forage together in groups. Each day, they leave their nocturnal roosts at dawn, often flying in V-formation to their daytime feeding areas in flooded fields, tidal mudflats, and freshwater marshes. Near sunset they return; hundreds and sometimes thousands crowding together into a relatively small area of marsh.

Field Identification

The ibis's distinctive long legs, neck, and beak and its dark maroon plumage, accented with metallic bronze and greenish iridescence on its sides, make it hard to confuse with any other prairie bird. In flight, its neck and legs are outstretched similar to cranes, as opposed to the folded-neck posture of herons and bitterns.

These male ibises fought for over a ❯
minute while an unconcerned female
foraged nearby.

Where to Find

Most commonly, the ibis frequents shallow marshes and sloughs, but groups sometimes move to flooded fields to forage.

Wintering Grounds

Large flocks winter in the coastal wetlands of Louisiana, Texas, and Mexico. In these same areas, but inland, they commonly target flooded rice fields. In a 1993 Christmas Bird Count in Crowley, Louisiana, 55,000 ibises were counted in such a habitat.

Diet and Feeding Habits

The white-face commonly forages in shallow wetlands where it probes the moist soil with its 12 to 14 cm- (4.5 to 5.5 in.) long bill searching for earthworms, leeches, crustaceans, frogs, dragonfly nymphs, and other larval insects. Near farmland, the birds are also attracted to alfalfa fields where they feed on spiders, snails, larval flies, and beetles. When prey is detected by the sensitive nerve endings at the tip of the bird's beak it elicits an instantaneous "snap reflex" closure of the bill.

Breeding Biology

The ibis is a relatively recent immigrant to Canada; the first ones were seen in the prairies in 1941. Beginning in 2006, ibises were reported nesting in Manitoba, Saskatchewan, and Alberta, with the greatest numbers observed in Alberta. Since then their range has expanded rapidly, and seasonal colonies are found on many prairie sloughs and lakes.

The white-faced ibis is seasonally monogamous, and birds may already be paired when they arrive in their colonies in spring. Courtship displays include mutual preening and head rubbing as well as entwining their necks and wagging about beakfuls of nest material. Ground nests of twigs, bulrushes, and cattails are made quickly by both partners in as little as two to four days and situated in thick stands of wetland vegetation, generally above shallow water. In large colonies, nests are closest together in the center, where they may be just 2 meters (6 ft.) apart, while those on the periphery are spaced 8 to 10 meters (26 to 32 ft.) from each other. Typically, three to four bluish green eggs are incubated for roughly 20 days, with males tending the nest in the daytime and females at night. Incubation begins soon after

the first egg is laid, so chick hatching is staggered. The pink-skinned nestlings are weak and uncoordinated and spend most of their time sleeping. Since they are only sparsely covered with brownish down they need to be brooded by an adult to prevent chilling. Chicks insert their head into an adult's mouth to feed on regurgitated food. Typically, the first-hatched chicks are the largest and outcompete their smaller siblings, so when food is limited the youngest chicks may not survive. By three weeks of age, the chicks are moving about and are fed away from the nest. By five weeks of age young ibis are making short flights; two to three weeks after that they are foraging independently up to a kilometer (0.6 mi.) away from the family nest.

The ibis's scientific name *Phegadis* ❯ comes from the Greek word for sickle in recognition of the bird's distinctive curved bill.

TUNDRA AND TRUMPETER SWANS
Cygnus columbianus and Cygnus buccinator

Family Details

Waterfowl Family (Anatidae), 156 species worldwide, 22 prairie species

Waterfowl, which include swans, geese, and ducks, are a group of large semi-aquatic birds, all of whom swim well and fly strongly. Waterfowl have a thick undercoat of down feathers, which the females pluck from their bodies to line and warm their nests. All young waterfowl are precocious when they hatch; their eyes are open, they are covered with fluffy down, and they are wound up for action. The young leave the nest almost immediately after hatching and follow their parents. From the beginning, the hatchlings feed themselves, although their parents may help them to locate food.

Prairie ducks can be divided into two broad categories: divers and dabblers. Watching how a particular duck feeds and how it takes flight will allow you to distinguish between the two groups. Dabblers either paddle along the top of the water, skimming food off the surface, or go bottoms up, stretching their necks under-water to reach food just below the surface. When dabblers take off, they jump straight into the air and are gone. This is the surest way to identify the dabbling group of ducks.

The diving ducks, as their name suggests, usually dive completely underwater when searching for food, and may remain submerged for up to a minute. These ducks have bigger feet than the dabblers, and their legs are positioned closer to the rear of their body, giving them more underwater power and steering ability. On land, however, the position of their legs produces an awkward gait. Diving ducks must take off from the water, running across the surface to build up speed before they become airborne.

Field Identification

Swans are large, long-necked, all-white birds with black beaks. The birds have no black on their wingtips as do snow geese and white pelicans. Although the trumpeter swan is the larger of the two species, the swans are difficult to distinguish in the field. At close range, a small yellow patch may be visible in front of the eyes of most tundra swans. Trumpeter swans, on the other hand, often have a red line on the upper edge of their lower bill.

Where to Find

Both species of swan are seasonal migrants that pass through the prairies in April and October. Tundra swans are the more numerous of the two. They nest in the Arctic and fly over the prairies during spring and autumn migrations. During migration, they often stop for a week or two in selected sloughs and lakes, to feed and rest. For example, thousands of tundra swans stop every year at Beaverhill Lake in Alberta.

Trumpeter swans are the largest and rarest swan in the world. No trumpeters nest in the prairies. The closest breeding areas are in northeastern British Columbia, the lakes in Alberta's Elk Island National Park, and the sloughs and lakes around Grande Prairie in west-central Alberta.

‹ A trumpeter swan may live up to 24 years in the wild, 33 years in captivity.

Wintering Grounds

Most of the tundra swans that wing their way across prairie skies spend the winter along the Pacific Coast, from Washington to California. In contrast, the primary wintering area for prairie trumpeters is a small area in Montana and Idaho.

Diet and Feeding Habits

Both species of swans eat a variety of aquatic plants. Their long necks and strong beaks enable them to reach down and uproot plants that smaller waterfowl, namely ducks and geese, are unable to reach. Swans also use their strong legs and the sharp claws on their large webbed feet to dig up underwater vegetation. When accompanied by cygnets, parent swans will paddle in place to flush uprooted plants to the surface where they are easier for the young swans to reach.

Breeding Biology

Both species of swans mate for life, pairing when they are three to four years old. The pairs show a strong attachment to their nesting grounds and return to the same area every year to raise their chicks. Trumpeters may even use the same nest several years in succession, adding new cattails, grasses, and reeds each breeding season until the nest mound becomes as large as a muskrat house. Swans are fiercely aggressive around their nest, and usually there is just one pair on each lake, unless the lake is very large. These short-tempered birds will attack intruders unmercifully. Swans readily chase geese and ducks out of their territories, and if they catch trespassers, they may trample and bite them repeatedly. In two reported incidents, tundra swans killed six-week-old goslings that accidentally strayed into their territories. The aggressive nature of these large, powerful birds helps them to protect their eggs and offspring from foxes, coyotes, ravens, and gulls.

Swans lay five or six eggs, which the female incubates alone for about a month. The cygnets hatch in June and are on the wing by late summer. The young swans migrate south with their parents in October.

→ **Trivia Tidbit**

By the turn of the century, trumpeter swans were nearly extinct, having been hunted relentlessly for food and feathers. By 1930, the only known breeding population was in Yellowstone National Park in Wyoming. There were also a few remnant flocks left in Montana, Alaska, and Alberta. As a result, a joint U.S. and Canadian restoration program was started, and trumpeter numbers slowly began to increase. Today, after nearly 90 years of protection, roughly 4,500 trumpeters migrate through southern Alberta annually, and continent-wide there are now over 46,000 of these magnificent swans.

⟨ As group size increases, there are more eyes to watch for predators, and a tundra swan can spend less time on vigilance and more time on feeding.

CANADA AND CACKLING GEESE

Branta canadensis and Branta hutchinsii

Family Details

Waterfowl Family (Anatidae), 156 species worldwide, 22 prairie species.

See Tundra and Trumpeter Swans for a general discussion of the Waterfowl Family.

Field Identification

The familiar Canada goose has a black head and neck with a large white cheek patch. In flight, the characteristic V-formation and the familiar honking makes this goose the best known of its kind. The subspecies that nests in the prairies is the "giant Canada," *Branta canadensis maxima*, the largest of the seven races of Canada goose in North America. An average male giant Canada weighs 5.5 kilograms (12 lb.), but some record holders have tipped the scales at twice that weight.

In 2004, mainly based on genetic differences, four races of Canada geese were recognized as belonging to a separate species, the cackling goose (*Branta hutchinsii*). The four races generally resemble Canada geese in appearance but are smaller and display slightly different plumage details. Cackling geese nest in the Arctic and migrate through the prairies in spring and autumn.

Where to Find

The geese frequent marshes, sloughs, lakes, and rivers throughout the prairies.

Wintering Grounds

Both geese winter on inland lakes and waterways in the southern United States, although some Canadas may remain in the prairies along large rivers that remain ice free and where there are nearby crop fields in which to forage.

Diet and Feeding Habits

The geese are vegetarians that savor the stems and shoots of sedges, grasses, and many aquatic plants. They also relish grain crops. Additionally, as every golfer knows, Canada geese love Kentucky bluegrass. The birds love it so much they always leave a special thanks for the greenskeeper to scrape off his boots. On land, both geese species feed by grazing as they walk along, and on the water they may upend like dabbling ducks or just submerge their head and neck to reach juicy underwater plants.

❰ A cackling goose may weigh just half as much as a nesting prairie Canada goose.

Breeding Biology

April flights of migrating geese brighten the hearts of everyone and herald the return of spring. Of the five species of geese that commonly fly over the prairies, only the Canada goose nests here. Nest building often begins in early May, and the finished product is a mound of vegetation hidden among cattails and bulrushes in shallow water or built on a small island for protection. Canadas also like to nest on top of abandoned muskrat and beaver lodges, and sometimes the geese will even use an old raptor's nest, setting up a high-rise homestead 15 meters (50 ft.) up in a tree. To avoid coyotes and foxes some Canada geese, along large prairie rivers, nest on inaccessible cliff ledges. The four to seven creamy white eggs hatch after about a month, and the adults immediately move their brood of golden goslings to the water for safety. The goslings stay with the parents all summer and may even accompany them on their autumn migration. Most Canadas have left the prairies by the end of October.

‹ The newly hatched goslings of Canada geese are preyed upon by ravens, crows and large gulls that will swoop down and snatch any youngster that strays from the safety of its parents.

SNOW AND ROSS'S GEESE

Chen caerulescens and Chen rossii

Family Details

Waterfowl Family (Anatidae), 156 species worldwide, 22 prairie species

See Tundra and Trumpeter Swans for a general discussion of the Waterfowl Family.

Field Identification

Both geese are white with black wingtips. Ross's geese are smaller than snows, weighing roughly a third less, and have a shorter neck, which gives them a different silhouette. At close range, the Ross's goose lacks the prominent dark "grinning" patch characteristic of the snow goose.

The snow geese that migrate through the prairies occur in two different color plumages, a light and a dark variation. Three-quarters or more of the birds are white, the remaining ones, the so-called "blue geese," have a white head and upper neck and a bluish gray body. White and "blue" varieties of snow geese mix freely, and flocks usually contain both color variations. Snow geese often fly in undulating lines. For this reason, some hunters call them "wavies."

Snow geese that have fed in coastal tidal areas frequently have the white feathers on their face stained a rusty orange by the iron minerals in the mud.

Where to Find

In April and early May, large flocks of white geese fly north over the prairies, returning again in late September and October. The geese may stop temporarily on large lakes to rest and feed during both their spring and autumn migrations. Some important staging areas in the prairies include Delta Marsh in Manitoba, the Quill Lakes in Saskatchewan, and Beaverhill Lake in Alberta.

Wintering Grounds

Both geese winter mainly along the Gulf Coast, from the Mississippi River southwest to Tampico, Mexico. Large numbers also overwinter in the Central Valley of California and in Bosque Del Apache Wildlife Refuge in New Mexico.

Diet and Feeding Habits

During migration over the prairies, the geese feed on newly sprouted grasses and waste grain in stubble fields.

Breeding Biology

Snow geese nest along the western coast of Hudson Bay and throughout the High Arctic. They are the most abundant goose in the Arctic, numbering in the millions, and commonly breed in large colonies on the open tundra. The largest colony, containing 460,000 birds, is on the Great Plain of the Koukdjuak on southwestern Baffin Island.

Ross's geese also nest along the western coast of Hudson Bay and in a few selected areas in the Canadian Arctic. Even so, over 90 percent of them breed in the Queen Maud Gulf Lowlands where the total population numbers over a million geese.

Both species of geese lay four to five white eggs. These are incubated mainly by the female while the male stands guard nearby. The goslings hatch after 24 days and are flying by the time they are seven weeks old.

→ Trivia Tidbit

Since the 1970s, the snow goose population has exploded and now exceeds five million birds. The dramatic increase has been destructive to the coastal habitats of the birds' Arctic nesting grounds. In spring, the geese feed by "grubbing" in which they remove divots of soil and vegetation to reach the nutrient-rich belowground parts of their favored plants. Grubbing destabilizes the soil, leading to accelerated erosion, vegetation loss, and habitat deterioration. As a result of this destructive foraging, lush intertidal salt marshes and coastal sedge meadows have been transformed into bare mudflats called "goose barrens."

‹ *(top)* A blue goose may mate with a white mate or another blue one.

(opposite) The distinctive head and bill › shape is the easiest way to distinguish between a Ross's goose (left) and a snow goose (right).

NORTHERN PINTAIL *Anas acuta*

Family Details

Waterfowl Family (Anatidae), 156 species worldwide, 22 prairie species

See Tundra and Trumpeter Swans for a general discussion of the Waterfowl Family.

Field Identification

The drake pintail is unmistakable. It sports a chocolate brown head and a long, slender white neck with a thin white line extending up behind its ear. Its sides and back are grayish, with black under its pointed tail. In flight, the trailing border of its inner wing, called the speculum, is iridescent bronze-green edged with white. The female's plumage is a cryptic mottled brown.

Where to Find

The pintail is widespread throughout the prairies. The duck favors shallow sloughs and marshes and semi-permanent wetlands, especially seasonally flooded fields.

Wintering Grounds

They winter along both continental coastlines and throughout the interior of Mexico and the southern United States.

Diet and Feeding Habits

Pintails are dabblers. During the breeding season, they eat mostly aquatic invertebrates: snails, crustaceans, fly larvae, water boatmen, and earthworms. They also dabble for seeds, especially those of grasses and bulrushes.

Breeding Biology

These elegant waterfowl are graceful, acrobatic fliers, and their courtship is a delight to watch. The males chase prospective mates in fast-wheeling "pursuit flights" that feature rapid dives from great heights and low, ground-hugging flight. These conspicuous aerial displays commonly involve two or three drakes following a single hen, but as many as 16 males may be in pursuit. The flights usually last less than four minutes, but the rare one may carry on for over half an hour. Pintails are among the earliest nesting ducks on the prairies. Writers Ray and Jim Salt summarized: "Before the end of April the female has concealed her nest in a meadow, under a bit of roadside brush, or in a cultivated field and is incubating her eggs when farm operations commence." Regrettably, thousands of pintail nests are accidentally destroyed during the routine burning and cultivation of stubble fields every spring.

The female alone incubates the clutch of seven to nine creamy yellow eggs and leads the ducklings to water when they hatch after 25 days. Pintails often build their nest far from water, and the downy ducklings may have to waddle 2 kilometers (1.2 mi.) or more to reach the safety of a slough or pond. The pintail family makes this dangerous journey at night when fewer predators are around.

→ Trivia Tidbit

Ducks and geese differ in a number of ways. Male ducks are typically brightly feathered, whereas female ducks are a drab, mottled mix of browns, tans, and grays. In contrast, male and female geese have similar plumage. Whereas ducks eat fish, crustaceans, aquatic insects, and plant life, geese are primarily vegetarians, and though geese are accomplished swimmers they do not always feed in the water, and many spend considerable time foraging in fields for grain and greenery.

One very big difference between ducks and geese is the strength of the pair bond. All prairie ducks mate with a different partner each year, and the pair bond typically breaks down soon after the eggs are laid. The female duck is a single mother from that point on. In geese, however, the pair bond is very strong, often lasting a lifetime. During the nesting season, the male goose assumes an important role in family duties. He defends the territory from trespassers, he may help to incubate the eggs, he guards the female while she incubates, and he accompanies the goslings on outings and protects them from predators. In autumn, geese migrate as a family. The faithful pair stay with each other on the wintering grounds and fly north together the following spring.

MALLARD *Anas platyrhynchos*

Family Details

Waterfowl Family (Anatidae), 156 species worldwide, 22 prairie species

See Tundra and Trumpeter Swans for a general discussion of the Waterfowl Family.

Field Identification

The male mallard is the most familiar of all wild ducks. Its metallic green head and neck, yellow bill, and chestnut breast make it unmistakable. In flight, its inner wings feature a violet patch bordered in front and behind by a strip of white. The female, as in all prairie ducks, is a mottled brown.

Where to Find

The mallard is one of the most widespread and adaptable species of ducks. It occurs wherever there is shallow water, either still or slowly flowing.

The familiar mallard has been introduced ❯ into Australia, New Zealand, and South Africa as well as multiple countries in South America.

Wintering Grounds

This duck is extremely hardy and winters as far north as there is open water, including many locations in the southern Canadian prairies. In Calgary, Alberta, where I live, tens of thousands of mallards winter along the Bow River, each day flying to surrounding croplands to feed on spilled grain.

Diet and Feeding Habits

The mallard dabbles for seeds, roots and stems of grasses, pondweeds, sedges, and other aquatic vegetation. It also eats tadpoles, frogs, crustaceans, and insects when an opportunity arises. Young ducklings need fats and proteins for growth, and they eat mostly aquatic insects during the early weeks of their life.

Breeding Biology

Pairs form in the late fall on the wintering grounds. Courtship involves bill dipping, head-flicking, and tail-shaking displays. Whistles, grunts, and quacks are thrown in for auditory accompaniment. Throughout the winter, the drake protects the hen from the bothersome attention of rival males. This allows her to build up greater fat reserves, which she will need for migration and nesting. In spring, the drake follows the hen back to the nesting grounds, often to the same area where she herself was hatched and raised. As in most ducks, the drake abandons his mate soon after the eggs are laid, and the hen is left on her own to incubate the clutch and raise the ducklings.

With so many idle "divorced" drakes loafing around, it is not surprising that forced copulations have been reported in mallards and many other species of waterfowl. Most of these aggressive attacks occur in the morning hours when eggs are most likely to be fertilized. Several males may attack at once, leaving the resident drake outnumbered and unable to defend his mate against them. Female mallards have even been killed during such "gang rapes."

→ **Trivia Tidbit**

The prairies are often called the "duck factory" of the continent, because more than half of all the ducks in North America are reared there. Eighty percent of all redheads, canvasbacks, pintails, and mallards start life on a prairie slough.

The cryptic plumage of the female ❯
mallard helps it avoid detection by
predators when it nests on the ground.

AMERICAN WIDGEON *Anas americana*

Family Details

Waterfowl Family (Anatidae), 156 species worldwide, 22 prairie species

See Tundra and Trumpeter Swans for a general discussion of the Waterfowl Family.

Field Identification

The widgeon is sometimes called the baldpate because of the conspicuous bright white crown on the male's head. This handsome drake also has an iridescent greenish patch on the sides of its head and sports rusty feathers on its sides. The female has a plain brownish body and a gray head. In flight, both sexes display a green speculum on their wings.

Where to Find

The widgeon is common on prairie ponds and sloughs.

Wintering Grounds

Most of these ducks migrate to the warmer climes of the extreme southern United States and farther south to the Caribbean and Central America.

Diet and Feeding Habits

The widgeon commonly dabbles in the shallow water and mud along the shoreline for the seeds and stems of grasses, sedges, rushes, and pondweeds. It is not a diving duck, but it still has a taste for many aquatic plants that are too deep for it to reach. The solution: piracy. I once watched a drake widgeon repeatedly attack an American coot every time it came to the surface with succulent plants it had torn loose from the bottom. Wigeons also bushwhack diving ducks, such as canvasbacks and redheads and steal their meals.

Breeding Biology

Widgeons are among the earliest ducks to arrive on the prairies, returning in late April and early May, shortly after the pintails and mallards. The widgeon, like most ducks, begins to breed when it is one year old. Pairs form on the wintering grounds and the drake follows the hen back to her chosen nesting area in the spring. Every season, the female has a different here-today-gone-tomorrow male partner, and she usually nests three or four times in her life. The hen, alone, builds a compact nest of grass and weeds, lined with down. Typically, the nest is found near water. The ducklings usually hatch after three and a half weeks and start to fly by the time they are six weeks old. Because they nest on the ground, the eggs of most prairie ducks are vulnerable to mammalian predators. Researchers in North Dakota found that 30 to 40 percent of widgeon nests were lost to keen-nosed mammals. As well, a five-year study in Alberta showed that four out of five widgeon nests were destroyed. In most cases, the egg-nappers were striped skunks.

(opposite) Numerous non-breeding ❯
species of waterfowl migrate through
the prairies in spring and autumn,
including the ring-necked duck
(upper left), bufflehead *(upper right)*,
common goldeneye *(lower left)* and
greater white-fronted goose.

❮ *(top)* The male widgeon can be readily
identified in flight by the large white
patches on its wings.

NORTHERN SHOVELER *Anas clypeata*

Family Details

Waterfowl Family (Anatidae), 156 species worldwide, 22 prairie species

    See Tundra and Trumpeter Swans for a general discussion of the Waterfowl Family.

Field Identification

The drake may sometimes be mistaken for a mallard since both ducks have a metallic green head. Other field signs to look for are a black "spoonbill," a conspicuous yellow eye, bright white breast, and rusty brown sides and belly. The brown cryptic coloration of the hen is similar to that of many prairie duck species, but her large orange-brown spoonbill is unique and relatively easy to spot.

Where to Find

Shovelers prefer shallow sloughs and marshes where there is submerged vegetation. They often select wetlands with an equal mix of open water and cattails or rushes where they can hide.

Wintering Grounds

"Spoonies" winter on inland lakes and marshes throughout the southern United States and Mexico.

❮ Six male shovelers, eager to mate,
  harass a solitary female.

Diet and Feeding Habits

All prairie dabbling ducks have a comb-like fringe along the edge of their upper and lower beaks, which they use to strain food from the water. The birds draw mud and water into their mouths and then force it out through this filtering system. Of all the dabblers, the shoveler has the finest straining system. It feeds on a variable mix of seeds and aquatic invertebrates, sieved from the water, though it tends to eat more animal food than most dabblers do. Common foods include seed shrimps, snails, and copepods, many of which can occur in great numbers.

I'll never forget how I learned about the abundant invertebrate life that lurks in the bottom ooze of a prairie wetland. I wanted to photograph shovelers, so I set up a blind in the shallow water along the edge of a small slough. Because I had forgotten my hip waders, I stripped down to my underwear and went barefoot, enjoying the feel of the cool mud around my ankles and the squish of soft muck between my toes. I spent several hours cramped inside the blind, and only toward the end of my vigil did I get an inkling that I had made a mistake. The next day my lily-whites were rosy-red, swollen, and covered with blistered, oozing bites. Nothing I did for days afterward seemed to ease the itch. I swear to you, unkind critters live in prairie mud, so give a cheer for the filter-feeding dabblers.

Breeding Biology

The northern shoveler is one of the last dabblers to breed. In the Canadian prairies, peak nest-building for them occurs in the last week of May. The details of egg-laying and incubation in the shoveler follow the general pattern common to most dabblers. Typically, the hen lays an egg every day, and once the egg is laid, she covers it and leaves the nest for the rest of the day. She returns in the middle of the night, lays another egg in the early morning hours, and then leaves again for the day. Most shovelers lay eight to 12 eggs in this way, and once the clutch is complete the female does all the incubation. During the 25 days of incubation, the hen usually takes just two breaks a day, one in the morning and another in the afternoon. Each break lasts about an hour and a half and gives the female time to eat, drink, and preen.

Hatching is highly synchronized in shovelers, as it is in all waterfowl. The young begin to chirp while they are still inside the egg, several days before they hatch. Researchers speculate that this prehatching communication helps the ducklings coordinate the timing of hatching. In shovelers, an entire clutch may hatch within four hours! Over the next seven weeks, the ducklings dabble, grow, and flap their way to independence.

‹ The widespread northern shoveler is one of the most common ducks on the prairies.

BLUE-WINGED TEAL *Anas discors*

Family Details

Waterfowl Family (Anatidae), 156 species worldwide, 22 prairie species

See Tundra and Trumpeter Swans for a general discussion of the Waterfowl Family.

Field Identification

The blue-winged teal is one of smallest prairie dabblers. With an average weight under half a kilogram (1 lb.), it takes three blue-winged teals to match the weight of a single mallard. The drake blue-wing is best identified by the distinctive white crescent on its dark blue face. In flight, the leading half of the duck's inner wing is pale blue, although it can appear whitish in poor light. Female blue-wings are a mottled brownish gray, and their small size is one of the better clues to their identity.

Where to Find

Blue-wings are one of the most common ducks on the prairies. They favor small, shallow ponds and sloughs, especially ones that have wet grassy meadows nearby.

After the breeding season, the male blue-wing, like all prairie ducks, molts its wing feathers and becomes flightless for a short time.

Wintering Grounds

These teal winter from the extreme southern United States on through Mexico and Central America to the northern countries of South America. One blue-wing banded in Delta Marsh, Manitoba, was later shot on a lake in Ecuador, 4,000 meters (13,000 ft.) above sea level, on the slopes of Cotopaxi Volcano. The little teal had flown at least 6,400 kilometers (3,975 mi.) to reach its wintering grounds. Another hardy blue-wing, banded in Saskatchewan, flew to a marsh in Peru, a distance of at least 11,300 kilometers (7,020 mi.). Apparently, blue-wings wintering in South America often migrate long distances over open water, an uncommon practice among dabbling ducks.

Diet and Feeding Habits

Three-quarters of a blue-winged teal's diet consists of the seeds of grasses and sedges and the stems and leaves of pondweeds. The rest of the time it eats beetles, bugs, caddisfly larvae, the nymphs of damselflies and dragonflies, amphipods, seed shrimps, and snails.

Breeding Biology

Pairs usually form on the wintering grounds or during spring migration, so most of the blue-wings have a partner by the time they reach the prairies. From the time females arrive on the nesting grounds until they start to lay, they are feathered feeding machines, spending 50 to 70 percent of the day eating. There is a good reason for this: a clutch of teal eggs can equal 80 percent of the female's weight, so a great deal of energy is required to produce them. If a hen loses her clutch to predators, she may nest again, often choosing a site within 50 meters (164 ft.) of her earlier nest. These so-called "replacement clutches" are usually smaller—a reflection of the high energetic drain imposed upon the female.

Like all dabblers, the drake blue-winged teal hangs around his mate just long enough to fertilize her and see her settled on the eggs, and then he leaves. The female incubates alone and stays with the ducklings for six to seven weeks until they finally fledge.

→ **Trivia Tidbit**

In mid-summer, all waterfowl become flightless for several weeks while they molt and replace their flight feathers. The birds are especially vulnerable to predators at this time, and many of them flock together on the open water of large lakes and sloughs. Some ducks, such as teal, stay hidden in cattails and bulrushes while they are molting and come out to feed in the open only at night. Northern shovelers are particularly shy when molting and stay hidden most of the time, feeding very little. As a result, they lose weight but regain it quickly in a late summer feeding binge that fuels them for their migration south.

∧ Preening cleans, oils, and removes parasites from feathers.

GREEN-WINGED TEAL *Anas crecca*

Family Details

Waterfowl Family (Anatidae), 156 species worldwide, 22 prairie species

See Tundra and Trumpeter Swans for a general discussion of the Waterfowl Family.

Field Identification

The green-winged teal is the smallest of the dabbling ducks. The male has a conspicuous cinnamon head with an iridescent green patch on the side running from its eye to a small crest at the back. From a distance you can almost always see a white vertical stripe on the side of its body in front of its folded wing. The mottled brown female is easily confused with female cinnamon and blue-winged teal. Its small size is the best way to differentiate them, albeit that can be a challenge.

Where to Find

Although both green-winged and blue-winged teal nest in the prairies, green-wings are more abundant in the north while the latter are more common in the south. Because of their small size and mode of feeding by tipping up, green-wings favor shallow sloughs and ponds. They like to preen and loaf along the shore and often sleep on one leg with their bill tucked under a wing. Both of these behaviors limit the loss of body heat that occurs more readily in birds with smaller bodies.

Wintering Grounds

Green-wings begin to leave the prairies in August, and most have moved on by the end of October. Early nesting males are the first to migrate, followed by late-nesters, then failed female nesters, and, finally, females with broods. Green-wings commonly spend the winter in the southern United States, the Caribbean, and Mexico.

Diet and Feeding Habits

Typically, these small dabblers feed near shore in shallow water, often where the water is less than 6 centimeters (2.4 in.) deep. When multiple ducks are feeding together the aquatic insects, mollusks, crustaceans, grass, and sedge seeds on which they feed become scarce, and the birds are forced to forage in progressively deeper water but rarely deeper than 12 centimeters (4.7 in.). They also feed on mudflats, probing the surface for invertebrates that live in the upper layers of the wet goo. The comb-like projections on the inner edge of their bill, called lamellae, are more finely spaced than in most dabbling ducks, so they are able to capture smaller invertebrates and seeds than most. Seeds comprise more than 90 percent of an adult's diet, but downy ducklings, as in all young waterfowl that need protein and fats to fuel their growth, eat mainly insect larvae, especially during the first month of their life.

Breeding Biology

Green-wings form pairs during winter, with up to 25 males courting a female, or several females, at the same time. Courtship is very similar in all the teal species and typically includes whistles and head movements. The head plumage in the different teal species is quite distinctive and striking; consequently, courting males show off these features to females with bobbing, nodding, and head-shakes. Successful males vigorously guard their mates from courtship by other males and will bite intruders and chase them away.

Green-winged teal nest on the ground, well concealed under thick vegetation, typically within 200 meters (656 ft.) of water. The male accompanies the female as she selects a nest site, but he does not assist in its construction. His primary concern, as with males of virtually all animal species, is to protect his paternity by preventing other males from mating with his partner. Egg laying occurs in May, although unusually cold weather may cause a delay. A female lays one egg a day until she has a complete clutch of six to nine eggs. She then adds down to the nest by plucking feathers from her breast and begins the 22-day incubation. Her mate abandons her as soon as she starts to incubate. Although ducklings can swim, dive, walk, and forage within a few hours of hatching they are susceptible to chilling, and the female broods them during cold weather and at night until they are several weeks old.

The male green-wing becomes ❯
sexually mature in its first winter.

CINNAMON TEAL *Anas cyanoptera*

Family Details

Waterfowl Family (Anatidae), 156 species worldwide, 22 prairie species

See Tundra and Trumpeter Swans for a general discussion of the Waterfowl Family.

Field Identification

The cinnamon teal is a fast-flier that has been clocked at speeds of 80 kilometers per hour (50 mph). This teal is a small dabbler, only marginally larger than the blue-winged teal. The drake is unmistakable with his rich chestnut head and body, deep scarlet eyes, and powder blue patches on his inner wings. The drake cinnamon teal is arguably one of the most beautiful ducks on the prairies. The female, a cryptic mix of gray and brown, is difficult to distinguish from the female blue-wing and green-wing, and when attempting identification, it is probably best to admit defeat and immediately move on to another bird.

Where to Find

The cinnamon teal prefers marshes, flooded ditches, farm ponds, and the shallow margins of sloughs and lakes. It uses alkaline lakes more than most dabblers. In prairie Canada, the cinnamon teal is less widespread than most dabblers and is found mainly in southern Alberta and southwestern Saskatchewan.

Wintering Grounds

Many of these teal spend the winter in the southwestern United States, Mexico, and northern Central America, although some travel as far as northern South America.

Diet and Feeding Habits

In many areas, 80 percent of a cinnamon teal's diet consists of plants, mainly the seeds, leaves, and stems of rushes, sedges, grasses, and pondweeds. Some of these foods can be difficult to digest. The teal, in common with most waterfowl, has a muscular gizzard located midway between its mouth and its stomach. Here, seeds and other tough foods are ground up with the help of gravel and grit that the birds swallow for this purpose. The gizzard of a bird is equivalent to the grinding molars of a mammal.

Breeding Biology

The courtship of the cinnamon teal takes place on the wintering grounds and includes an array of displays: chin-lifting, head-pumping, and pursuit flights. The pursuit flights usually involve a couple of chattering drakes chasing a solitary female. Cinnamon teal are extremely agile in flight, making sharp turns and fast, low-level passes. Shortly after a pair arrives on the spring breeding grounds, the male selects and defends a small territory of about 30 square meters (323 sq. ft.) or less. In most cases, the territory includes the nest site and a loafing area, which the drake uses while the hen is on the nest. In typical dabbler fashion, the drake cinnamon teal abandons his mate by the third week of incubation and goes off to molt. The hen does all the incubation and cares for the ducklings.

A substantial portion of cinnamon teal nests, as many as a quarter of them, may be parasitized by other ducks. It is probably easy enough for another hen to sneak into a nest and lay an egg while the unsuspecting owner is away foraging. In a Utah study, redheads were the most common parasites, but other culprits included ruddy ducks, the northern shoveler, and the northern pintail. Cinnamon teals, however, are not always the victims; sometimes they are the offenders. Teals will parasitize the nests of others of their own kind and will also occasionally leave an egg with an unwary mallard.

→ **Trivia Tidbit**

Until very recently, the waterfowl habit of eating gravel and grit caused the deaths of as many as three million ducks, geese, and swans every year. The cause: lead poisoning. For decades, the lead pellets from shotgun shells accumulated on the bottoms of prairie wetlands. For every duck killed by a hunter, it was estimated that 1,400 pellets (almost a quarter of a kilogram or half a pound) settled on the bottom of a slough. The fine lead pellets were ingested incidentally when the birds were feeding or were swallowed intentionally as grist for their gizzards. The lead from a single pellet was enough to poison a duck. In 1997, it finally became illegal to fire shotgun shells filled with lead pellets over any wetland or waterway.

⟨ During the summer molt, the male ⟩
cinnamon teal loses its distinctive rusty
feathers and resembles the mottled
brown female.

REDHEAD AND CANVASBACK

Aythya americana and Aythya valisineria

Family Details

Waterfowl Family (Anatidae), 156 species worldwide, 22 prairie species

See Tundra and Trumpeter Swans for a general discussion of the Waterfowl Family.

Field Identification

Both redheads and canvasbacks are diving ducks that submerge when feeding and run across the water's surface to become airborne. The two divers have similar plumage: rusty heads, black chest, and whitish gray sides and back. Identification relies mainly on the head and bill shape, which are strikingly different. The canvasback has a long sloping forehead and a large all-black bill, whereas the redhead has a round head, a steep forehead, and a blue bill tipped with black. The females of both species are drab colored, with varying amounts of brown and gray. For both sexes, the characteristic head profile of the two ducks is usually enough to distinguish them. Once you acquire this kind of expertise you can no longer consider yourself a casual duck watcher; you are a serious duckaholic.

⌃ A mother redhead constantly watches for danger from aerial predators, such as hawks and gulls when it leads its ducklings to feeding areas.

❮ *(opposite)* Male redhead (left) and canvasback (right) in spring breeding plumage.

Where to Find

Redheads and canvasbacks are common throughout the prairies. They are found on lakes, marshes, and sloughs, especially those bordered by bulrushes and cattails, which the ducks favor for nesting cover.

Wintering Grounds

The greatest numbers of these divers winter in sheltered coastal waters off California and in the Gulf of Mexico. Hundreds of these ducks may gather in large offshore rafts to loaf, sleep, and feed.

Diet and Feeding Habits

Aquatic plants are the staple food of canvasbacks and redheads, though both ducks also feed on mollusks, midges, caddisflies, and other insects. When I first began to watch prairie ducks I wondered how so many different species could share the same slough and not seriously compete with one another. The answer: habitat partitioning. By feeding in slightly different ways, in slightly different areas of the slough, and on slightly different foods, the various ducks lessen the competition among them. For example, the dabblers feed in the shallows and the divers in deeper water. The canvasback and redhead illustrate how subtle this partitioning can be. Both are diving ducks that commonly feed in open water up to 3 meters (10 ft.) deep, but when necessary the slightly larger and heavier canvasback can dive to depths of 10 meters (33 ft.). The bill structure of the two ducks also differs. The redhead's beak is better designed to strain aquatic insects than is that of the canvasback, which is specialized for sieving plant foods. Finally, the two ducks commonly feed at different levels of the water column. Canvasbacks plunge to the bottom, tear out roots and tubers, and sieve the mud for seeds. Redheads, on the other hand, feed more on submerged stems and leaves from mid-water levels.

Breeding Biology

The basic breeding pattern is the same in diving ducks as it is in dabblers. Courtship and pairing occur on the wintering grounds or during spring migration. Once the birds arrive on the nesting grounds, the drake dutifully defends his mate from other males while she eats, eats, and eats, and then lays her eggs. His intentions, mind you, are totally selfish, as guarding the female is the best way to ensure his paternity. With the six to ten eggs laid, the drake promptly deserts his partner, and the hen is left to incubate the clutch by herself and care for the ducklings.

Canvasbacks and redheads, as in all diving ducks, build their bulky reed nests over standing water, usually less than a meter (3 ft.) deep, and hide them in thick stands of emergent cattails and bulrushes. This is quite different from the behavior of dabbling ducks, which typically nest on land, at times several kilometers from the nearest water. The main reason for the difference is anatomy. Dabblers walk well on land and can take off from a jumping start, so it is easy for them to nest away from water. By doing so, they also have a larger area in which to hide their nests from predators. Diving ducks, with their legs positioned farther back on their bodies, have difficulty walking on land and usually require a run across the water to become airborne. For both these reasons, they are tied to wetlands for nest sites.

‹ *(opposite)* Female redhead *(left)* and canvasback *(right)*.

RUDDY DUCK *Oxyura jamaicensis*

Family Details

Waterfowl Family (Anatidae), 156 species worldwide, 22 prairie species

See Tundra and Trumpeter Swans for a general discussion of the Waterfowl Family.

Field Identification

The ruddy is a unique prairie duck belonging to a worldwide group of small diving ducks called "stiff-tails." The drake has a rusty neck and body; a black head with large white cheek patches; a sky-blue bill; and a long, stiff tail that sometimes points straight upwards. The brownish female is best identified by her stubby size and stiff tail. On takeoff, ruddy ducks patter across the water and beat their short wings so fast they are sometimes called "bumblebee ducks."

Where to Find

Ruddies are usually one of the last prairie ducks to return in the spring. They are relatively common on marshes and sloughs, and they prefer wetlands that have a lot of emergent vegetation poking above the water. Ruddy ducks do not seem to like large areas of open water.

Wintering Grounds

The greatest concentrations of ruddy ducks occur in saltwater lagoons, marshes, and bays along the Pacific coast of Mexico. In some winters, the birds may be highly localized. This happened one year near Acalpulco, Mexico, when 107,000 ruddies were counted offshore. At the time, this may have been more than a third of all the ruddy ducks in North America.

Diet and Feeding Habits

Ruddies, like so many prairie ducks, eat a mixed diet of aquatic plants and insects, including diving beetles, dragonfly nymphs, water boatmen, amphipods, and the larvae of midges and caddisflies.

Breeding Biology

The courtship of this attractive duck is amusing to watch. The cocky little drake could easily be mistaken for a windup toy, especially when he performs his "bubbling" sequence, the major display used by courting males. In Volume 3 of Handbook of North American Birds, the display is described in great detail. "The drake sits high in the water, neck swollen, head held as high as possible, with his tail angled forward so that its tip is near his nape. Then the head is drawn down 6 to 12 times in increasing tempo and, each time, the bill is slapped against the breast producing a hollow tapping sound … the bill striking the feathers near the waterline forces air from among the feathers into the water and bubbles form around the breast." More than 40 bubbling displays may be performed by a single male in just 20 minutes. It seems the vigor and frequency of the bubbling display reflects the dominance of the male. Conclusion: top drakes really bubble.

Their nest is a floating platform of plant materials anchored to cattails or rushes. Sometimes the ducks will use an old coot nest or an abandoned muskrat house. When water levels are unstable and neighboring nests become flooded, a nest that is still high and dry may be used by multiple females. In one such "dump nest" a researcher found 80 eggs. Typically, a clutch of six to eight eggs is laid in June and is incubated entirely by the female. Once the ducklings hatch, the hen stays with her brood for three to four weeks, then leaves to molt.

→ **Trivia Tidbit**

The ruddy duck probably has more regional names than any other prairie duck. Some of the more colorful ones include "batter-scoot," "noddy," "cock-tail," "hickory-head," "paddy-whack," "quill-tailed coot," "sleepy dick," "rudder bird," "hard-headed broadbill," "dumpling duck," and "bumblebee buzzer." One book listed 70 different common names. It's easy to understand why researchers use scientific names to avoid confusion.

The "bubbling" display of the ❯
male ruddy duck.

TURKEY VULTURE *Cathartes aura*

Family Details

New World Vulture Family (Cathartidae), 7 species in North and South America, 1 prairie species

Vultures are large soaring birds with broad wings. The family includes the Andean condor of South America, one of the largest flying birds in the world. Large male condors can weigh up to 15 kilograms (33 lb.) and have a wingspan over 3 meters (10 ft.). The vultures are nature's cleanup crew and feed almost entirely by scavenging the bodies of dead animals. They rarely kill prey themselves.

Field Identification

The expression "beautiful from far, but far from beautiful" is how I would describe the turkey vulture. At close range, the bird's featherless head covered with wrinkled red skin is hard to find attractive. In flight, however, the vulture's true beauty literally soars. Rising aloft on a plume of warm air, the turkey vulture is a graceful, skilled aeronaut. I have watched them float, seemingly effortlessly, for nearly an hour and never flap a wing. The broad V flight profile of this large dark bird, seen especially when it banks on a turn, is the surest way to distinguish the turkey vulture from any of the soaring hawks on the prairies.

❮ The featherless head of the carrion-
eating turkey vulture enables the bird to
shunt blood to cool itself, advertise its
mood and motivation to fight, as well
as keep itself clean.

Where to Find

The turkey vulture, known colloquially by birdwatchers as TV, is an uncommon breeder in the southern prairies. It can be seen drifting aloft along remote stretches of the Red Deer, Milk, and South Saskatchewan Rivers. Since the 1950s, turkey vulture numbers have risen all across the northern edge of their range in Canada. The increase in sanitary landfills and road-killed animals is thought to be the reason for this.

Wintering Grounds

Turkey vultures are long-distance soaring migrants. Most prairie breeders probably winter from Mexico to northern South America. They often travel great distances without eating and are masters of energy conservation. To save energy, they migrate only by day when favorable thermals and air currents can carry them onward with as little effort as possible. One spring, I watched a northward procession of turkey vultures soar overhead in Costa Rica. In a two-hour period, several thousand vultures drifted past.

Diet and Feeding Habits

The claws of a turkey vulture are blunt and its feet are rather weak and ill-adapted for grasping prey. As well, the bird's beak,

‹ With its large wings a turkey vulture can soar with a minimum of energy.

though sharp-edged, is not a killing weapon. For all these reasons, the vulture feeds primarily on carrion, although on their wintering grounds they sometimes prey on hatchling sea turtles. As a rule, the bird is a shy, patient diner and never rushes to feed on a carcass. After all, there is no need to hurry, and if the animal on the menu is not quite dead, it is better to wait for its demise and avoid any accidental injury. The best guarantee for a safe meal is the sweet scent of putrefaction. Turkey vultures are one of the few birds with a well-developed sense of smell. In fact, the vulture probably locates most carcasses by scent rather than vision. In the 1930s, petroleum engineers in Texas pumped ethyl mercaptan (the smelly substance wafting from carcasses) into natural gas pipelines. By watching the behavior of local turkey vultures the oilmen could quickly locate leaks in the pipeline.

Breeding Biology
I once found a vulture nest in the Cypress Hills of Saskatchewan. The bird had chosen a small cave on a hillside, a common nest location. The vultures also nest on cliff ledges and in hollow stumps or logs. Beginning in the early 1980s, vultures were even found nesting in deserted houses in Saskatchewan. This behavior increased dramatically in the 1990s and eventually spread to Alberta as well. In a study conducted in Saskatchewan between 2003 and 2006, turkey vultures nested in abandoned houses 126 times.

The nest I found in the Cypress Hills held two gray chicks, which is the usual number for a pair to raise. Turkey vultures may mate with the same partner several years in succession and may pair for life. The birds usually arrive on the prairies in early May and leave again sometime in August.

→ **Trivia Tidbit**
To cool itself, the turkey vulture urinates on its own legs. The evaporation of the watery whitewash lowers the bird's body temperature. In one experiment, an overheated vulture repeated this messy maneuver 40 times in four hours. As distasteful as this behavior seems, bear in mind that every manual of desert survival advises humans to rub urine on their limbs to cool themselves.

This vulture chick hatched in the ⟩
attic of an abandoned barn.

GOLDEN EAGLE *Aquila chrysaetos*

Family Details

Hawk and Eagle Family (Acciptridae), 233 species worldwide, 8 prairie species

This large family is comprised of the diurnal birds of prey: hawks, eagles, kites, and harriers. The members range in size from huge eagles to small robin-sized sparrowhawks. The female is usually larger than the male, a reverse from the typical situation in birds. In some cases, the female may be 50 percent heavier than her mate and have noticeably larger talons and beak.

Hawks and eagles rely on keen eyesight, perhaps four to eight times more acute than humans, to locate prey. They use three main methods to hunt: aerial stalking, soaring, and patient perching. All hawks and eagles have sharp talons and kill their prey by lethal penetration.

Field Identification

The large size alone—female wingspans can reach 2.3 meters (7½ ft.)—distinguishes the golden eagle from every other prairie bird of prey except perhaps a juvenile bald eagle, which is also big and has dark feathers. The plumage of the adult golden eagle is dark brown all over, and the golden feathers on the nape of its neck are usually only visible at close range. It takes three to four years for a juvenile eagle to acquire full adult plumage. While it is maturing, a juvenile can be identified by a broad white area at the base of its tail and white patches on the undersides of its wings.

Where to Find

The majestic golden eagle is an uncommon resident of native grasslands, badlands, and undisturbed river valleys throughout the northern prairies.

Wintering Grounds

Some eagles may leave their prairie breeding grounds, but many stay year-round. Those that leave probably migrate to grassland and desert areas farther south in the United States. Eagles banded in prairie Saskatchewan have been recovered in winter in Kansas, Colorado, and Texas. Another young eagle banded in Dinosaur Provincial Park in Alberta migrated and spent the winter hunting in South Dakota.

Diet and Feeding Habits

These regal raptors primarily hunt small mammals: ground squirrels, prairie dogs, jackrabbits, cottontails, and occasionally young deer and pronghorn. In a Wyoming study, during the winter months from November through February, researchers watched golden eagles attack seven pronghorn, killing three. In each case, a solitary eagle targeted herds of pronghorn, containing 120 to 350 animals. Once the pronghorn detected the hunting eagle they clumped together closely and fled as a group. All the attacks were similar, with the eagle landing on the racing victim's back or neck and riding it, sometimes for 200 meters (656 ft.), until the hapless animal and the eagle collapsed together on the ground. At one kill, a second eagle arrived within eight minutes, and after 27 minutes, five eagles were feeding on the kill. The four pronghorn that escaped, all with bleeding wounds, ran back to

❮ Like many birds of prey, the golden eagle adds fresh greenery to its nest throughout the breeding season.
Photo © Jon Groves

their fleeing herd and their fate was unknown. Eagles also hunt grouse, pheasants, ravens, and magpies. One nest I examined in southwestern Saskatchewan had cormorant remains in it. Golden eagles will also eat snakes, especially bullsnakes, and even venomous prairie rattlesnakes. Carrion is eaten anytime but is more important in the birds' winter diet, and they readily steal prey from other predators, such as red foxes, great horned owls, bald eagles, and prairie falcons.

Breeding Biology

Golden eagles may not begin to breed until they are several years old; in some cases not until they are age six or seven. Lifelong monogamy is the rule, but as in most animals studied, some pairs divorce after one or more seasons. A breeding pair defends a combined hunting and nesting territory, the size of which depends upon the abundance of prey. In a study in the densely occupied Snake River Canyon in Idaho, the eagles had territories of just 29 square kilometers (11 sq. mi.). Eagle territories on the Canadian prairies have not been studied so their size is unknown.

Courtship begins as early as late March and early April and includes "sky-dancing" in which one eagle, or both, fly up and down in an undulating course. Most often they nest on cliff ledges and steep badland slopes, and an undisturbed pair may use the same site year after year. Successive generations of golden eagles occupied one nest site for 250 years, from 1689 to 1938—a record! Each year the birds add new sticks to their nest, called an aerie, and it can become massive. The largest nest on record was found in Sun River, Montana, and measured 16.1 meters (53 ft.) tall and was 2.59 meters (8.5 ft.) wide. Although a female eagle may lay up to three eggs, rarely four, the pair seldom raise more than a single chick.

Sometimes the adults may stock a nest with a substantial larder of prey. At one nest in Saskatchewan, bird-banders found two adult white-tailed jackrabbits, a Richardson's ground squirrel, a burrowing owl, a juvenile black-billed magpie, and a large fish. At another nest they recorded two adult and two juvenile jackrabbits, four ducks, and a long-tailed weasel. Young eagles make their first flight at around 65 days of age after several weeks of wing-flapping and hopping about the nest. The adults, primarily the male, continue to feed fledglings for several months after they leave the nest.

❮ *(left)* These eagle chicks were feeding on the carcass of a cormorant. *(right)* When an eagle mantles over prey it raises the feathers on its head and neck to intimidate rivals and discourage theft.

BALD EAGLE *Haliaeetus leucocephalus*

Family Details

Hawk and Eagle Family (Acciptridae), 233 species worldwide, 8 prairie species

See Golden Eagle for a general discussion of the Hawk and Eagle Family.

Field Identification

The adult bald eagle is unmistakable with its dark body and all-white head and tail. Juveniles acquire full adult plumage when they are five or six years old. As they grow, young eagles are a variable patchwork of dark and light feathers, and at this stage they can easily be confused with a golden eagle.

Where to Find

Bald eagles are seen in the prairies mainly during their spring and autumn migrations to and from the northern forests, although sometimes they overwinter. Ice-free areas in large rivers are attractive wintering sights. Up to 34 eagles, for example, winter annually along the Bow River in Calgary. Farther south, in the United States, important eagle wintering sites include Monte Vista Wildlife Refuge in Colorado, Quivira National Wildlife Refuge in Kansas, and Squaw Creek National Wildlife Refuge in Missouri.

Wintering Grounds

Migrants passing through the prairies winter mainly in the southern United States. Birds banded in a northern Saskatchewan study wintered in Arizona and Texas.

Diet and Feeding Habits

Anyone who has ever watched a nature documentary on bald eagles knows that the birds eat fish in the summer. Their winter diet, however, is less well known. Like many birds of prey, the "noble" bald eagle will scavenge dead animals: winter-killed deer, pronghorn, and livestock. Two or three eagles may gather and squabble at a single carcass. One winter, I surprised a juvenile bald eagle feeding on a road-killed mule deer beside the Trans-Canada Highway. Another eagle was dead on the ground nearby. The dead bird probably collided with a vehicle as it tried to fly away. Bald eagles will also readily steal a kill from other birds of prey. In the croplands around Calgary, wintering bald eagles commonly pilfer the dead ducks killed by gyrfalcons and prairie falcons. Other winter foods include jackrabbits, cottontails, and waterfowl. One April, I watched an adult bald eagle kill a female mallard that was feeding in a small area of open water in an ice-covered lake. It dragged the struggling duck to shore and ate it alive.

Breeding Biology

Most bald eagles nest along the shorelines of northern lakes in large stick nests at the tops of trees. The eagles return to their breeding grounds as soon as the ice melts, usually in late April and early May, and leave again just prior to freeze-up in October. These familiar raptors mate for life, and a pair returns to the same territory, and often the same nest, year after year. The time from egg laying to fledging of the young takes about four months.

→ Trivia Tidbit

Both bald and golden eagles can lay up to three eggs, but in most cases only one or two young survives, depending upon the abundance of food brought to the nest. When food is scarce, the largest chick bullies its siblings and gets most of the food. In some cases, the biggest eaglet may even attack and peck its smaller nestmates and kill them. The parent birds never interfere in these family squabbles, and the dead chicks are eaten by the family or are simply trampled into the nest.

The impressive weaponry of a mature ❯ bald eagle includes a large, hooked beak and heavy, sharp talons.

NORTHERN HARRIER *Circus cyaneus*

Family Details

Hawk and Eagle Family (Acciptridae), 233 species worldwide, 8 prairie species

See Golden Eagle for a general discussion of the Hawk and Eagle Family.

Field Identification

Harriers are a subgroup of raptors with long narrow wings and a long tail. Their slow, buoyant flight pattern is quite characteristic—a repeating sequence of flap-and-glide close to the ground. Male northern harriers are pearl-gray above and white below, and the females, as much as 50 percent heavier than their mates, are brown above and tan below with dark streaking. In both sexes, the most noticeable field sign is a bright white rump patch.

Where to Find

The northern harrier is widespread throughout the prairies. This handsome raptor was formerly known as the marsh hawk, a reflection of the bird's common breeding habitat, though it also frequents rangeland, croplands, and wet prairies.

A hunting harrier, such as this female, > typically tacks back and forth close to the ground.

Wintering Grounds

Most harriers abandon the prairies in October. They continue to hunt on their southward migration, moving between 15 and 100 kilometers (9 and 60 mi.) a day. Their wintering range extends from the central United States, through Mexico, and into Central America as far as Panama. Harriers return to the northern prairies in late March and April with adult males arriving first.

Diet and Feeding Habits

The facial feathers on the harrier form a disk, giving them a distinctly owl-like appearance. Harriers rely heavily on hearing to capture prey, as do many owls. The sharp-eared raptors hunt mainly small rodents but will also take songbirds, frogs, snakes, and insects, such as grasshoppers. One time, in southern Alberta, I watched an adult white-tailed jackrabbit repeatedly run and jump at a low-flying male harrier that was swooping back and forth overhead. When I went closer to investigate, I found three newborn leverets huddled together on the ground. There was a small patch of fresh blood on the grass nearby. Apparently, the harrier had caught one of the young hares earlier and had returned for another. Another time, I saw a female harrier hold a female blue-winged teal underwater until it drowned, a relatively large prey for this species of hawk.

Breeding Biology

Harriers nest on the ground, and I have found a number of them in cattail marshes and also in thickets of rose and snowberry bushes out on the dry prairies. In most cases, the hawks have a different mate every year, and when vole numbers are especially high they show a strong tendency for polygyny: a single male pairing with two females. On rare occasions, an older male may take up to five female partners!

A female harrier does all the incubation, while the male feeds her. In doing this, some males may catch more than 40 voles in a single day! Harrier chicks hatch after a month or so. For the first week, the female stays with the young continuously, shading them from the heat of the sun and brooding them when it is cold and wet. During this time, the male provisions the entire family. Usually, the food deliveries are passed on the wing, and it's exciting to see. The male flies high and drops the prey to the female, who catches it deftly with her taloned foot while cruising in the air beneath him. At seven days of age, the chicks are about three times as large as when hatched, and from then on both parents hunt to feed the rapidly growing family. During the month before the chicks fledge, a brood of three may receive 388 meals, totaling 28.5 kilograms (63 lb.) of prey—enough crop-eating voles and mice to warm any farmer's heart.

The pearly grey male harrier rarely > shares in incubation.

FERRUGINOUS HAWK *Buteo regalis*

Family Details

Hawk and Eagle Family (Acciptridae), 233 species worldwide, 8 prairie species

See Golden Eagle for a general discussion of the Hawk and Eagle Family.

Field Identification

The ferruginous is the largest and heaviest hawk in the prairies, and at a distance it can sometimes be confused with an eagle. The adult has a bright rusty back and rump, white chest and belly, and rusty leggings that form a distinct V against the bird's light underparts. It's the only hawk with a clean white underside on its tail.

Where to Find

This shy, open-country bird of prey favors badlands and native grasslands. Grazing, cultivation, and the poisoning of small mammals has caused its widespread decline across the prairies. In Canada, the ferruginous hawk is a threatened species and breeds only in the southern portions of Alberta and Saskatchewan.

Wintering Grounds

This beautiful hawk overwinters in the deserts and grasslands of northern Mexico and the southwestern United States from California to Texas.

Diet and Feeding Habits

The ferruginous hawk is a specialist predator of small- to medium-sized mammals including jackrabbits, cottontails, ground squirrels, prairie dogs, and pocket gophers. It commonly hunts from an elevated perch making a short glide of less than 100 meters (328 ft.) to strike its prey. The method it uses to capture pocket gophers is particularly interesting. Author Dwight Smith described the technique in *Handbook of North America Birds, Volume 5.* "Pocket gophers push up earthen piles while tunneling. The hawk flies slowly until it discovers a fresh damp pile. Then it alights and waits for a gopher to push close to the surface; then the hawk rises a few feet in the air and comes down stiff-legged onto the loose earth to [capture] the gopher … " It's unknown whether the hawk uses auditory clues to catch its prey in the same way an owl listens and pounces on the snow to capture a mouse underneath.

Breeding Biology

During courtship, pairs often soar at high altitudes, and the male performs flight maneuvers described as "sky dancing" in which he flaps with slow, deep, exaggerated wing beats, pitching up and down. This may be followed by repeated steep dives and climbs. The pair sometimes fly with their legs dangling and may interlock talons and spiral toward the ground.

Ferruginous hawks frequently use a nest from a previous season. The bird is extremely wary and even someone innocently inspecting the nest site, during the building phase or during egg laying and early incubation, may be enough disturbance to cause the bird to desert.

Over the years I have noted the different nest sites chosen by ferruginous hawks in the badland country of southern Alberta. The two most popular locations are the tops of lone trees and ground nests on the upper edges of steep clay slopes. The nest platforms I have examined (in the autumn after the nesting season) were usually made of branches and sticks with an inner cup of dried grass. In rangeland, dried chips of cattle dung were often added to the nest. Ground nests can be a meter (3 ft.) or more in diameter and some were that tall. Only golden eagles construct stick nests as large as some of those of ferruginous hawks. In the 1800s, ferruginous nests were sometimes made of bison bones and lined with the wool of these shaggy prairie beasts.

Pairs establish breeding territories in early April, and by early May they are incubating. The usual clutch contains two to four eggs, but the number varies from one to eight depending upon the abundance of prey. The female broods the chicks for three weeks, and after that she helps the male hunt prey for the young. Within two weeks of fledging, the young hawks begin to hunt for themselves, though their parents continue to feed them for several weeks afterward.

‹ *(lower left & right)* This ferruginous nest on a steep badland slope held five chicks *(see red arrow)*. *(upper right)* Young hawks may abandon the nest before they are strong fliers and become temporarily grounded as a result.

SWAINSON'S HAWK Buteo swainsoni

Family Details

Hawk and Eagle Family (Acciptridae), 233 species worldwide, 8 prairie species

See Golden Eagle for a general discussion of the Hawk and Eagle Family.

Field Identification

The Swainson's hawk is one of the most common soaring hawks on the prairies. When in flight, the field signs to look for are a dark-headed bird with a brown upper chest and white or creamy underwings and belly. Usually, it also has a dark band visible near the end of its tail. A dark color variation occurs in roughly 10 percent of these hawks, which have dark brown underwings and belly instead of the usual white.

Where to Find

This bird is an open-country raptor, widespread throughout farming country. The range of the Swainson's hawk overlaps that of the red-tailed hawk and the ferruginous hawk. The three raptors lessen competition among themselves by selecting slightly different prairie habitats. The ferruginous prefers badlands and dry rangelands, the red-tail favors the aspen woodlands of coulees, and the Swainson's is found most often in agricultural lands bordered with bushes and trees.

❮ This juvenile Swainson's hawk was drying its wings after a summer downpour.

Wintering Grounds

The Swainson's hawk is the marathon migrant among North American birds of prey. Some individuals may make annual round-trip journeys of 22,000 kilometers (13,700 mi.), commuting between prairie Canada and the pampas of northern Argentina. To conserve energy on these long journeys the hawks masterfully exploit thermal updrafts and favorable winds. Each day as the sun heats the Earth, columns of warm air rise to the sky. The hawks spread their broad wings and slip into these rising currents to be carried aloft. Hundreds of hawks may circle together to form a "kettle," with some birds circling clockwise and others counterclockwise. At the top of the updraft, as high as 6,000 meters (19,700 ft.), the air cools and loses its lift, and one by one the hawks break out of the circle and glide off in the direction they wish to travel. From one updraft to another, the birds circle and glide their way thousands of kilometers across the plains, deserts, and rainforests that separate their breeding and wintering grounds. One female Swainson's from Saskatchewan was tracked by satellites. She left Canada on September 22 and arrived in Argentina 69 days later.

Diet and Feeding Habits

Anytime I have seen a Swainson's with prey in its talons, the unlucky victim was always a Richardson's ground squirrel. On the birds' summer breeding grounds, these tawny little rodents are the number one food, though the hawks also eat pocket gophers, songbirds, and snakes. Swainson's hawks nest a few

weeks later than other prairie hawks, and the timing coincides perfectly with the emergence of young, naive ground squirrels.

Breeding Biology

The Swainson's hawk often builds its flimsy nest of branches and Russian thistle in the top of tall willow bushes on the edge of a field. The shelterbelts surrounding abandoned farmhouses are another popular nest site. Swainson's don't seem to mind living relatively close to humans. In an Alberta study, nearly a quarter of the nests were within 0.5 kilometers (0.3 mi.) of a farmyard.

Adult males establish nesting territories near the same area where they hatched, and they defend these aggressively. They patrol from great heights and will dive on any feathered trespassers, attempting to rake them with their talons. If an intruder sees the dive coming he may roll in midair and lock talons with the attacker. The pair, locked in combat, then spirals to the ground. In most cases, the combatants in these territorial dogfights separate unscathed, but sometimes there are lacerations, broken wings, and, on rare occasions, fatal head injuries. The irascible male Swainson's does not limit his aggression to males of his own kind. He may also attack trespassing ferruginous and red-tailed hawks, northern harriers, turkey vultures, golden eagles, great horned owls, crows, and imprudent wildlife photographers.

In a typical year, the monogamous pair raises two young, which fledge in late July.

❮ *(top)* Fresh green leaves may aid in nest sanitation and deter parasites by releasing natural volatile chemicals. *(bottom)* The feet of a young hawk are equipped with needle-sharp talons.

ROUGH-LEGGED HAWK *Buteo lagopus*

Family Details

Hawk and Eagle Family (Acciptridae), 233 species worldwide, 8 prairie species

See Golden Eagle for a general discussion of the Hawk and Eagle Family.

Field Identification

The rough-leg is a lemming-hunting specialist that nests in the Arctic tundra and migrates to the prairies in winter. It derives its common name from its heavily feathered legs. The hawk's relatively small beak, an adaptation to small rodent prey, gives its head a distinctive appearance. The features I always search for in identifying this handsome Arctic hawk are dark underwing wrist patches and a white base to the underside of its tail.

Where to Find

This hawk prefers open, treeless areas including wet meadows, cultivated fields, pastures, and native grasslands.

(opposite) The eye color of the juvenile ❯ rough-leg gradually changes over several years from pale yellowish to dark brown.

(right) The rough-legged hawk's ❯ scientific name, Buteo lagopus, means the hare-footed buzzard.

Wintering Grounds

The rough-leg naturally gravitates to winter habitat that resembles its treeless tundra breeding grounds and is found in open country from southern Canada throughout the western and central United States. It arrives from the Arctic in October or November and leaves in mid-March to early April, although I have seen them delay their Alberta departure until the early days of May when red-tails, ferruginous, and Swainson's hawks have already returned to the prairies.

Diet and Feeding Habits

On the prairies, wintering rough-legs hunt primarily voles and mice and occasionally northern pocket gophers, muskrats, and weasels. Typically, they hunt from an elevated perch, such as a power pole, haystack, fence post, or tree. In windy weather, when the energetic costs of hovering are lessened, rough-legs may combine periodic hovering with soaring. When they locate prey while hovering they may interrupt their descent several times, with their feet dangling, before dropping with outstretched legs onto their target. In one study of wintering rough-legs in Ohio, the birds hovered three times in an average descent before pouncing on prey. During a typical prairie winter, an adult rough-leg will catch around four to six small mammals each day. On their summer nesting grounds while feeding growing chicks a pair of adults may catch as many as 900 collared lemmings to feed themselves and two ravenous nestlings.

It's well known that predators and prey are in a constant arms race to outmaneuver each other, and in the case of rough-legged hawks versus lemmings the tactics are especially interesting. To begin with, the feces and urine of lemmings are especially visible in ultraviolet light. It turns out that rough-legs, unlike humans, can see this part of the electromagnetic spectrum and use their ultraviolet sensing ability to monitor rodent activity and concentrate their hunting efforts. Lemmings counter this threat by seasonally changing the location of their latrines. In winter, under a protective mantle of snow, lemmings locate their latrines on top of the ground, but in summer when they are most at risk of being detected by a hungry hawk they use underground latrines to hide the ultraviolet evidence of their activity. As one biologist quipped, lemmings in summer use "indoor plumbing."

Breeding Biology

Pairs may establish a bond on their wintering rounds, then migrate together to their Arctic breeding grounds. On the Arctic tundra where there are no trees, the hawks either nest on level ground or on the steep slopes of hillsides and river valleys. They build a bulky nest of sticks, most of which are gathered by the male and arranged by the female. Construction may take three to four weeks to complete. On average, rough-legs lay a clutch of three eggs, but researchers in Nunavut have found nests with as many as seven, although the survival of so many nestlings would occur only when the lemming cycle is at a peak and prey is super abundant. Nest failure is high in areas with many predators, such as grizzly bears, Arctic foxes, wolves, wolverines, and snowy owls. As well, storms and winds destroy many nests when hillsides slump. In an Alaska study, 20 percent of nests were lost because of such muddy landslides.

As is typical of most birds of prey, the female rough-leg does most of the month-long incubation while her mate provisions her. Afterward, the female broods the chicks nearly continuously for about three weeks and her mate feeds the entire family. With 24 hours of daylight, the male may hunt 15 to 18 hours a day. Young rough-legs can fly weakly at five to six weeks of age, but the fledglings continue to depend on their parents for food possibly until they migrate south for the winter.

RED-TAILED HAWK *Buteo jamaicensis*

Family Details

Hawk and Eagle Family (Acciptridae), 233 species worldwide, 8 prairie species

See Golden Eagle for a general discussion of the Hawk and Eagle Family.

Field Identification

The underside of the red-tailed hawk is quite variable in color, ranging from cream to rufous to dark chocolate brown, making it difficult to identify until it flies off or circles in the distance. The bright rusty upper surface of its tail is unmistakable. The adults give a recognizable two- or three-second scream resembling a steam whistle. Hollywood loves the cry of this hawk and has used it in many films whenever an atmosphere of wilderness is needed, often in settings where no self-respecting red-tail would be found.

Where to Find

The adaptable red-tailed hawk is commonly seen all across North America in a wide variety of forest habitats. In the prairies, it is found wherever there are groves of tall aspens in which to nest. Usually, the red-tail prefers habitats with more trees, and taller trees, than do Swainson's, although both hawks hunt in open country.

Wintering Grounds

The red-tail, like the other common hawks of the prairies, is absent for six months of the year. It winters all across the central and southern United States and northern Mexico.

Diet and Feeding Habit

Most of the time, this hawk hunts from the top of a tree, scanning the surroundings with its sharp eyes. Hares, rabbits, ground squirrels, ducks, songbirds, and bullsnakes are all on the menu. When quarry is spotted, the hawk silently drops from its perch and flap-and-glides swiftly toward the victim. When the hawk is just 2 to 3 meters (6½ to 10 ft.) from impact—a mere millisecond—it swings its legs forward and strikes the prey, usually with a single taloned foot. It is not uncommon for larger prey, especially those with sharp teeth, to struggle and bite the hawk. The legs and feet of many red-tails bear the scars of these struggles.

Breeding Biology

The red-tail, like so many large raptors, may use the same nest several years in a row, adding new sticks each season. During nest building, egg laying, and incubation, the pair continues to add fresh aspen branches and other greenery to the nest, sometimes on a daily basis. The purpose of this greenery is unclear, but a number of explanations have been proposed. Fresh green leaves may advertise ownership of a nest and deter trespassers. The leaves may sanitize the nest by covering waste materials, or the foliage may deter parasites by releasing noxious aromatic chemicals.

The family life of the red-tail is similar to that of other prairie hawks. The female does most of the incubation while the male provisions her. The clutch of two or three eggs hatches after about a month, and the chicks are then brooded by the female for another week or so while they become more resistant to the vagaries of the weather. By the time the young hawks are five weeks old, both parents are hunting to feed their voracious appetites. Young red-tails begin to fly when they are six or seven weeks of age, but require another six or seven weeks to learn to hunt and feed themselves.

After spending the winter in the ❯
southern United States, some red-tails
return to the prairies as early as the
end of March.

PRAIRIE FALCON *Falco mexicanus*

Family Details

Falcon and Caracara Family (Falconidae), 64 species worldwide, 5 prairie species

The scavenging caracaras, most of which live in South America, are slow-flying birds of prey that resemble vultures in their lifestyle. The falcons, on the other hand, are fast-flying aerial hunters. Once a falcon locates prey from the air, it descends on its target in a feather-rippling dive called a stoop. It strikes with a powerful blow of its clenched feet or with a deadly slash of its talons. If the victim is still alive, the falcon ends the ordeal with a lethal bite to the base of its skull using a specialized "tooth" called a tomial tooth on the edge of its upper beak. The tomial tooth is used like a wedge to force apart the vertebrae, injuring or severing the spinal cord. Raptor researcher Dr. Tom Cade believes this beak specialization allows the falcons to kill prey larger than they could otherwise tackle.

Field Identification

The prairie falcon is light brown above and whitish underneath with contrasting dark "armpits." The head and back of the prairie is much lighter than that of the peregrine falcon with which it may be confused. The prairie falcon's flight is usually low, strong, and fast.

❮ Falconry dates back thousands of years and has developed a specialized vocabulary. The nest of a bird of prey, such as this prairie falcon nesting in a sandstone cavity, is called an eyrie (pronounced EYE-ree)

Where to Find

This falcon is a denizen of open country, favoring native grasslands, rangelands, and badlands. This remarkable raptor is found throughout the northern prairies.

Wintering Grounds

Some of these attractive falcons remain on the prairies throughout the winter, but many migrate to the plains, deserts, and canyonlands of the western United States.

Diet and Feeding Habits

This versatile predator uses a number of hunting techniques: perch-and-wait, soaring followed by power dives from altitudes of 1,000 meters (3,300 ft.) or more, and low-level flapping flight to flush prey. In the latter, flight is fast and "contour-hugging," sometimes as low as 3 meters (10 ft.) above the ground. Occasionally, a crafty falcon will follow a northern harrier from aloft and steal its kill or capture escaping birds that are flushed by the harrier. In summer, on the Canadian prairies, the common prey of this falcon is primarily ground squirrels; secondarily songbirds, especially horned larks, mourning doves, and meadowlarks. When winter comes and the ground squirrels disappear into hibernation burrows, the adaptable falcon becomes strictly a bird hunter, targeting overwintering horned larks, snow buntings, and ducks. Albertan Jon Groves, photographer and falcon expert, has videotaped many prairie falcons killing ducks in winter. Females, being 30 to 40 percent heavier than males, are the only ones that have enough brawn to tackle hefty waterfowl. An average female prairie weighs roughly 0.9 kilograms (2 lb.), whereas a wintering mallard feeding in croplands on spilled grain may weigh around 1.2 kilograms (2.6 lb.). Jon has seen a female prairie kill a mallard with a single blow to its head. At other times, perhaps when the falcon's aim is off, or when the duck makes an evasive move at the last minute, it may take a dozen strikes to finish the job. No matter, such predation is a dramatic example of the killing potential of a prairie falcon's foot blows.

Breeding Biology

A mating pair may associate on their wintering grounds and then return independently in March to the northern prairies, males arriving a week or two before their partners. In a mild winter, pairs may arrive three to four weeks earlier. The most common nesting site is a bare cliff ledge with some degree of overhang for protection from inclement weather, located at least 9 meters (30 ft.) up, but not too close to the top where it could be reached by a nimble-footed coyote or fox. Less frequently, the falcon lays its eggs in the abandoned stick nests of other species, especially those of golden eagles and ravens. As is typical of all falcons, the prairie adds no material to its nest and simply lays its eggs on the bare ground, usually in a shallow depression scraped from available loose debris.

When ground squirrels are abundant, falcon pairs may nest close to each other. Researchers have documented nests that were just 36 meters (125 ft.) apart, although the average ranges from 0.5 to 1 kilometer (0.3 to 0.6 mi.), and the nest ledges are usually not in direct sight of each other. The mated pairs actively defend the area close to their nests but share a common hunting area with neighboring falcons.

In the Alberta prairies, the average falcon lays four to five eggs, one of the largest clutches of any prairie bird of prey; only the burrowing owl will sometimes lay more eggs. Incubation begins in early May, with the white downy young hatching roughly a month later. Although the female does all the incubation at night, male participation in the daytime varies greatly, ranging from zero help to taking on three-quarters of the daytime egg-warming duties. Once the eggs hatch, however, the female does all the brooding of the vulnerable nestlings while the male hunts for the entire family. When the male brings prey to the nest he passes it to his mate who then feeds the young. After a month, the parents simply drop food on the nest ledge and the young feed themselves. By six weeks of age, the young falcons are able to fly, but they continue to be fed by their parents for at least three weeks after that. A major danger to young fledglings is predation by great horned owls, which prey on the unsuspecting birds that naively roost on exposed ledges at night. In the end, three-quarters of the young die in their first year, most from starvation. The surviving yearlings return the following spring but usually do not breed for at least another year.

Biologists have seen prairie falcons carry dry cow manure in their talons, throw it in the air, and then catch it again before it falls to the ground. Such play behavior in birds of prey is a way for them to practice and develop survival skills. By chasing each other they build muscles and endurance, by manipulating objects they learn the dexterity needed to handle prey, and by engaging in aerobatic flight maneuvers they learn agility and fine control over their wings and tail. Increasingly, researchers also admit that sometimes raptors may play for no other reason than the sheer fun of it. Examples of play in birds of prey include peregrine falcons making mock attacks on inanimate objects, such as old animal bones; rough-legged hawks soaring, diving, and playing tag in twos and threes; red-tailed hawks repeatedly dropping sticks in flight, swooping down, and catching them again; and Swainson's hawks and golden eagles repeatedly releasing dead prey in midair and then diving after it before it reaches the ground.

❮ Often, as soon as a parent returns with prey, one of the chicks grabs it, turns its back on its siblings, and aggressively guards its meal.

❮ *(opposite)* These four-week-old prairie falcon chicks are gradually replacing their natal down with juvenile feathers.

This handsome male kestrel was hunting ❯
grasshoppers that periodically flushed
from the grass.

AMERICAN KESTREL *Falco sparverius*

Family Details

Falcon and Caracara Family (Falconidae), 64 species worldwide, 5 prairie species

See Prairie Falcon for a general discussion of the Falcon and Caracara Family.

Field Identification

The kestrel, smaller than a blue jay, is the smallest bird of prey in North America. The male and female kestrel differ in coloration, an uncommon trait in birds of prey. The larger female has a rusty back and wings, while her smaller mate has blue-gray wings and a rusty back. Both sexes have a characteristic pair of black streaks on the sides of their face. The birds also have two dark spots on the rear of their neck. It's speculated that these "eye spots" may deter predators from making a rear attack. The kestrel's habit of bobbing its head makes these eye spots even more convincing.

Where to Find

The kestrel was formerly one of the most common birds of prey in North America, but their numbers have been slowly declining in the last three decades. One possible culprit is our tireless war against insects, and in the words of noted ornithologist David Bird, "using pesticides with reckless abandon." Many prairie insectivorous birds, besides kestrels, are experiencing similar declines: meadowlarks, bobolinks, common nighthawks, loggerhead shrikes, and swallows.

When you are lucky enough to see a kestrel it is generally in open terrain, including fields, rangelands, and badlands. The kestrel commonly perches on telephone wires and fences.

Wintering Grounds

Some kestrels may overwinter in the Canadian prairies, but many migrate to the southern United States. Recently, there is an increasing tendency for urban kestrels to stay in Canada for the winter. An abundance of easy prey, in the form of house sparrows and starlings, enables the little falcons to fuel themselves against the cold.

Diet and Feeding Habits

The kestrel may either still-hunt from an elevated perch or hover-hunt. Hover-hunting is the most entertaining technique to watch. When prey is sighted, the falcon begins to hover and line up the attack. Usually, it is no higher than 25 meters (82 ft.). Sometimes, the bird may drop a few meters and continue to hover at a lower height, waiting for its prey to be more vulnerable. Kestrels can hover like this for up to a minute, or longer when the wind speed is high, but the energy costs are expensive. When the moment is right, the falcon drops like a rock and grasps its prey.

When I started to bird-watch 60 years ago, everyone called the kestrel the "grasshopper hawk" because of its appetite for these insects. On the prairies, this dexterous little falcon commonly catches the large red- and yellow-winged grasshopper species as well as dragonflies, beetles, butterflies, crickets, and wolf spiders. It also hunts songbirds, voles, mice, and bats.

Breeding Biology

The American kestrel may be the smallest bird of prey, but it has the largest sexual appetite. One pair mated 10 times in an hour. Another couple mounted 14 times in just 36 minutes. Researchers estimate that a pair may copulate 690 times in a season, even though twice a week would be often enough to fertilize the eggs. It's likely that frequent copulation reinforces the bond between the pair, a strategy that also seems to apply to our own species.

Kestrels usually nest in cavities. They may choose rock crevices in lofty cliffs, abandoned woodpecker holes, or natural hollows in aspen and cottonwood trees. Both parents incubate the clutch of four to six eggs, but the male's participation varies between individuals. In some cases, the male may incubate for as much as four hours, doing a morning and an afternoon stint. In other instances, he may sit on the nest only at night. The eggs hatch after about 28 days.

Raptor researchers Noel and Helen Snyder observed, "Like the young of many hole-nesting birds, young kestrels are relatively noisy, apparently deriving considerable security against predators from the nature of their nest sites." The young falcons first fly and leave the nest at one month of age, but they may return to the cavity at night with their mother for several weeks afterward.

PEREGRINE FALCON *Falco peregrinus*

Family Details

Falcon and Caracara Family (Falconidae), 64 species worldwide, 5 prairie species

See Prairie Falcon for a general discussion of the Falcon and Caracara Family.

Field Identification

The adult peregrine is a large falcon, dark gray on top and heavily barred on its undersides. The bird's head and face are dark, and it has distinctive "sideburns" on the sides of its neck. Female peregrines are larger and around 30 percent heavier than males; otherwise the sexes are similar in appearance. Juveniles are brown above and buff underneath with heavy streaking and also have the dark sideburns.

Where to Find

Historically, peregrines nested on cliffs along most of the large rivers in the northern prairies. After World War II, the indiscriminate use of the pesticide DDT gradually poisoned the birds. They failed to reproduce, and their numbers slowly declined. In 1975, the falcons were officially declared "extirpated" south of the boreal forest and east of the Rocky Mountains. Since then, the use of DDT has declined worldwide and captive-bred peregrines have been successfully reintroduced into the Canadian prairies, with many pairs choosing to breed in the urban core of cities, such as Calgary,

Edmonton, Saskatoon, Regina, and Winnipeg. The urban settings were sometimes chosen for release sites to lessen the danger from great horned owls, which often prey on young peregrines.

In 1995, wild peregrines finally nested again in the native Canadian prairies along the Red Deer and Bow Rivers in Alberta after an absence of nearly 30 years. In recent years, the adaptable peregrine has also repopulated the western regions of Montana, Wyoming, and Idaho as well as the Colorado Plateau.

Wintering Grounds

The exact wintering range of the prairie peregrine is not well known, but it is likely that most of the birds migrate to Mexico and Central and South America. Nestlings banded in Alberta have been recovered as far south as Belize, Venezuela, and Brazil. The photograph of the nesting falcon that appears here was taken on the 15th-floor ledge of a high-rise building in the center of Calgary in June. Dr. Gordon Court, a wildlife biologist with Alberta Environmental Protection, told me the remarkable story about this bird. Two years earlier, researchers noticed mysterious black electrical tape wrapped around the band on the bird's left leg, and they captured it to investigate. Under the tape, a condom wrapper contained a slip of paper with the name and address of a German shipping company. The biologists were intrigued and wrote to the company in Bremen, Germany, to unravel the story. Apparently,

one of the company's ships had been 160 kilometers (100 mi.) offshore from Tampico, Mexico, during a November hurricane, and the falcon had taken refuge on the ship. A Filipino seaman who loved birds had captured the falcon and taken it to his cabin to shelter the bird from the storm. Before releasing it he had attached the message to its leg.

Diet and Feeding Habits

The fast-flying peregrine is a versatile aerial hunter, and at one time or another has probably preyed upon every small- and medium-sized bird on the prairies. Urban peregrines commonly hunt pigeons, starlings, robins, and house sparrows—birds that do well in heavily populated human environments. The big-city peregrines surprised Dr. Court with some unexpected quarry: American coots, eared grebes, red crossbills, soras, blue-winged teal, and even escaped budgies and cockatiels. Dr. Court thinks a foraging falcon may hunt as far as 40 kilometers (25 mi.) from its nest, reaching the agricultural lands and wetlands that surround most cities.

The peregrine is so beloved by falconers because of one of its hunting strategies: the feather-rippling power dive called a stoop. An attacking falcon tucks its tapered wings and falls like a thunderbolt from the floor of the sky. In such a dive, the peregrine is the fastest bird on wings, reaching a recorded speed of 390

This female peregrine is brooding her young >
on a high-rise building in the center of Calgary,
Alberta, a city of one and a half million people.

kilometers per hour (242 mph). The victim is killed with a smashing blow from the peregrine's semi-clenched feet or is slashed to death with its trailing rear talons. In the coastal wetlands of Mexico's Baja California I've watched hunting peregrines strafe wintering flocks of willets and marbled godwits. Both of these shorebirds commonly migrate north to nest in the prairies. Another time, in the same region of Mexico, I accidentally flushed a great horned owl from a crevice in a desert arroyo. The owl was carrying a freshly killed peregrine falcon. Clearly, the predatory peregrine doesn't always have its own way.

Breeding Biology

Most peregrines are back on the prairies aggressively defending their nesting territories by the middle of April. The birds can be extremely faithful to their nest site, returning year after year. One female used the same location on a building, in downtown Edmonton, Alberta, for 12 years in a row.

Typically, a peregrine nest is nothing more than a scrape on the ledge of a cliff or a high-rise building. The birds usually lay three or four rusty speckled eggs that are among the most beautiful of raptor eggs. The female does most of the incubating, and for the 33 days it takes for the eggs to hatch, the male does much of the hunting and feeds his mate. Young peregrines begin to fly at around 40 days of age, but their parents feed them for at least four weeks afterward.

⟨ *(opposite)* This juvenile peregrine is feeding on a duck *(left)* The bare yellow skin at the base of a peregrine's beak is called the cere, the purpose of which is unclear.

RUFFED GROUSE *Bonasa umbellus*

Family Details

Grouse, Pheasant, Partridge, and Turkey Family (Phasianidae), 180 species worldwide, 10 prairie species

This large family includes grouse, pheasants, partridges, and turkeys. All might best be described as chicken-like birds that spend most of their time on the ground. They are reluctant fliers. All have relatively small wings for their body size, so their takeoffs are noisy, and flushed birds explode into flight with a roar of wings. Once on the wing, they fly close to the ground with bursts of rapid wingbeats, and they usually land after only a short time in the air.

The grouse, in particular, evolved in the cold climates of the Northern Hemisphere and all are superbly adapted to endure the worst winter weather. They have thick, dense plumage, comprising as much as 20 percent of their body weight. They also have protective feathers over their nostrils and on their legs and toes. In winter, they grow a fringe of scales along the edge of their toes called pectinations that increase the surface area of their feet and function like snowshoes.

Field Identification

The plumage of all the prairie grouse is a mottled mixture of earth tones, and one of the easiest ways to separate the species is by the appearance of the bird's tail. The ruffed grouse has a finely striped tail with a broad black band near the tip. The black neck "ruff" of the grouse, from which the bird derives its name, is present in both sexes, but it is usually hidden and is most visible in males during spring courtship.

Where to Find

The ruffed grouse is widespread throughout Canada. The bird's range corresponds almost exactly with that of two species of deciduous trees: the quaking aspen and balsam poplar. In the prairies, the grouse is a frequent inhabitant of coulees and streamside woodlands.

Wintering Grounds

The ruffed grouse is a year-round resident of the prairies, and most spend the entire year within a relatively small home range, usually less than 10 hectares (25 ac.). Adult males are particularly sedentary. They may spend their entire lives within a 200-meter (650-ft.) radius of their main drumming log.

Diet and Feeding Habits

The most important winter foods of the ruffed grouse are aspen buds and catkins, which is no surprise given the birds' close association with these trees. During the rest of the year, the grouse eat the buds, flowers, leaves, and berries of more than 500 kinds of plants. Young grouse chicks need great amounts of fat and protein to fuel their growth and eat large numbers of insects and spiders as well.

Breeding Biology

The drumming of the male ruffed grouse in early April is familiar to everyone who walks through a coulee after the cold, quiet days of winter. The drumming is produced by the rapid beating of the bird's wings against the air. A typical drumming session lasts seven to 10 seconds and is repeated, on average, every four minutes. Popular drumming sites are tree roots and old fallen tree trunks, and the same site may be used year after year for as long as the grouse lives. A human can hear a "drummer" half a kilometer (0.3 mi.) away, and I always thought it must be easy for a great horned owl, one of the grouse's main predators, to listen and locate the birds. It turns out, however, that the frequency of the grouse's drumming is below the hearing range of the owl.

After a female is lured to a drumming log and mates with the owner, the male ruffed grouse has nothing more to do with her. The female lays nine to thirteen creamy eggs in a shallow scrape under shrubbery or in some bushes and incubates them without any help for 23 days. An incubating hen spends more than 90 percent of her time on the nest, leaving only two or three times a day to feed. In late May, the chicks hatch, and within a day the female leads them away from the nest. The young grouse feed themselves from the moment of hatching, and they stay with their mother until the family breaks up in early autumn.

〈 As soon as a female appears near a drumming male, he fans his tail, raises the ruff on his neck, and struts around her hoping to make an impression.

〈 (opposite) Male ruffed grouse are true homebodies. Once a male acquires a territory he may spend his entire life within 200 meters of his main drumming log.

The vibrancy of a male's yellow combs ❯
and purple throat sacs are a reflection of
his health and vitality - cues a female can
use to evaluate him as a potential mate.

❮ Prairie sharp-tails can endure winter
temperatures as low as -40C (-40F).

SHARP-TAILED GROUSE *Tympanuchus phasianellus*

Family Details

Grouse, Pheasant, Partridge, and Turkey Family (Phasianidae),
180 species worldwide, 10 prairie species

*See Ruffed Grouse for a general discussion of the Grouse,
Pheasant, Partridge. and Turkey Family.*

Field Identification

The sharp-tail's name is a clue to the easiest way to identify
this cryptically colored prairie bird. The grouse has a pointed tail
with white patches on the edges, visible when the bird flushes.
The male and female are similar in appearance except during
courtship when the males pump themselves up and display
engorged yellow eye combs and vibrant purple throat sacs.

Where to Find

The sharp-tail is found throughout the northern prairies. It favors
open grasslands mixed with shrubbery, such as prairie rose, snowberry, and wolf willow.

Wintering Grounds

The sharp-tailed grouse is a year-round prairie resident. In winter,
the birds form flocks of up to 100 birds.

Diet and Feeding Habits

About 90 percent of the grouse's diet consists of the fruits,
seeds, flowers, and buds of plants. Less common foods include
beetles, grasshoppers, and crickets. Insects are most important
to young chicks and compose the bulk of their diet for the first
four to six weeks of life.

Breeding Biology

Grouse are one of my favorite groups of birds, and every spring
I try to witness the courtship of at least one of the family. Many
years ago, I wrote these words in *Windswept: A Passionate
View of the Prairie Grasslands*:

> In the Great Sand Hills of south-western Saskatchewan
> March is an empty time. The landscape is leached of
> color, and the bite of winter lingers as deer and pronghorn
> move slowly, rationing their strength. Silence pervades,
> the insects are locked in hibernation, and the songbirds
> are still a month away. The ground is frozen and brittle
> underfoot, the plants firmly held in check. But on a
> grassy knoll, life refuses to be restrained, and the sharp-
> tails dance. Each spring, sharp-tailed grouse assemble
> on ancestral dancing grounds to re-enact their courtship
> ritual. The males coo, cluck and strut. With their heads
> down and their tails pointed to the sky, they rapidly stomp
> their feet, and little clouds of dust erupt around them. The
> birds vibrate across the ground like wind-up toys; they run
> feverishly for a moment, and then suddenly stop.

Thirty or 40 males may gather on a dancing ground half the size of
a football field. Each male defends his own small patch of prairie.

One by one, female grouse wander through the cluster of males,
assessing the dancers for qualities only they can detect, looking
for a mate. Once the hen makes her choice she mates just once
and then leaves.

Sharp-tails nest on the ground, and every nest I have found
was hidden in a clump of rose bushes or snowberry. The hen
lays 10 to 13 plain, buff-colored eggs. As in all grouse, the eggs
hatch within hours of each other and the precocious chicks
are led away from the nest by the female. The down-covered
young are a mottled patchwork of gold, brown, and black and
blend perfectly with the dried grasses of the prairie. The young
become independent by two months of age.

➔ Trivia Tidbit

A clutch of grouse, pheasant, or waterfowl eggs usually hatch
within hours of each other. Remarkably, the chicks of these
birds synchronize their hatching by clicking to each other while
they are still inside the shell. In mallard ducks, for example,
older chicks that are about to hatch click at a rate between two
and 60 times per second. This relatively slow rate stimulates
the younger chicks in the clutch to get cracking and accelerate
their hatching efforts. Younger chicks, on the other hand, click
at higher rates, usually over 100 times per second. This, in turn,
slows down the struggles of the older chicks who, as a result,
may delay breaking free for more than 33 hours. The mechanisms of the natural world are sometimes truly extraordinary.

GREATER SAGE-GROUSE *Centrocercus urophasianus*

Family Details
Grouse, Pheasant, Partridge, and Turkey Family (Phasianidae), 180 species worldwide, 10 prairie species

See Ruffed Grouse for a general discussion of the Grouse, Pheasant, Partridge, and Turkey Family.

Field Identification
The greater sage-grouse is the largest grouse in North America. A large male can weigh over 3 kilograms (6.5 lb.), five times as much as a ruffed grouse. The bird's size alone is usually enough to identify it as well as its long tail feathers and black belly.

Where to Find
The sage-grouse lives in the driest areas of the northern prairies wherever expanses of sagebrush grow. In the American plains, the greatest numbers occur in Wyoming, Idaho, and Montana. In Canada, the grouse is limited to the extreme southwestern corner of Saskatchewan and the southeastern corner of Alberta, an area referred to as Palliser's Triangle. Sadly, sage-grouse numbers in Canada have plummeted in recent decades, and this handsome grouse is now designated as critically endangered. Biologists estimate there are fewer than 300 breeding birds remaining in the country. Some of the measures implemented to hopefully bolster the dwindling population include a captive breeding program with the subsequent release in 2018 of 34 adult sage-grouse; oil and natural gas wells in critical areas capped and the habitat reclaimed; power lines rerouted or buried because power poles are used by golden eagles that prey on the grouse; derelict buildings removed to eliminate habitat for chick and egg predators, such as ravens, great horned owls, and skunks; and, since 2011, 118 female sage-grouse captured in Montana and relocated to Alberta. The ultimate success of all these measures depends upon there being enough suitable sagebrush habitat to support a viable population. Otherwise the program will fail and sage-grouse will eventually disappear from Canada.

Wintering Grounds
The sage-grouse is a year-round resident of the prairies. In winter, it concentrates wherever exposed sagebrush is found.

Diet and Feeding Habits
The sweet scent of sagebrush on a summer morning is one of the great pleasures of a walk on the short-grass prairies. This aromatic plant is nutritious, retains its leaves throughout the winter, and is tall enough to reach above the snow. For these reasons, the leaves of sagebrush constitute nearly 100 percent of the winter diet of the sage-grouse. At other times of the year, the grouse eats the leaves of grasses and wildflowers as well as small numbers of ants, grasshoppers, and beetles. The grinding gizzard of the sage-grouse is less muscular than it is in the ruffed and sharp-tailed grouse, and as a result the sage-grouse eats fewer seeds and grains than either of these birds.

❮ *(top)* A dominant male in the center of a lek courts a trio of females. *(bottom)* In Wyoming, where sage grouse are more plentiful, over 50 males may display together on a single dancing grounds.

❮ *(opposite)* Male sage grouse do not acquire full breeding plumage until they are two years old. The tail feathers of an immature male are tipped with white and more blunt than those of a mature male.

Breeding Biology

From March to May, male sage-grouse cluster, as do sharp-tails, on traditional dancing grounds, called leks, to display and court females. Each male defends a small territory, sometimes less than 15 meters (50 ft.) across. The handsome suitor spreads his tail, struts, and inflates a large pendulous throat pouch. In the last moments of the display, the air trapped inside the pouch is suddenly released, producing two large pops—the grouse version of a satisfied burp. The central territories of a dancing grounds are occupied by the oldest, most dominant males, and for a sex-crazed male, the center of the lek is definitely the place to be. In one instance, a dominant male mated 37 times with 37 different females in 37 minutes. Ninety percent of the hens will mate with the few males displaying in the center of the lek. In fact, in a given year, nine out of 10 males never lay a feather on a female. They strut and pop in vain and, like many incurable sports fans, they dream of next season.

Female sage-grouse, like all prairie grouse, are single mothers. After the male contributes his three seconds of involvement, the hen is on her own. Typically, sage-grouse lay seven or eight eggs in a shallow nest at the base of a cluster of sagebrush. Any ground nest is highly vulnerable to mammalian predators, and up to 60 percent of sage-grouse eggs get eaten by badgers, coyotes, and ground squirrels. The hen incubates the eggs alone for 26 days and afterward stays with the chicks until they disperse later in the summer.

RING-NECKED PHEASANT *Phasianus colchicus*

Family Details

Grouse, Pheasant, Partridge, and Turkey Family (Phasianidae), 180 species worldwide, 10 prairie species

See Ruffed Grouse for a general discussion of the Grouse, Pheasant, Partridge, and Turkey Family.

Pheasants differ from grouse in having featherless legs and feet and no feathers around their nostrils. They all have strong legs and prefer to walk and run rather than fly. As well, no pheasant has the characteristic colorful inflatable air sacs present in grouse, although many species have vibrant wattles and combs. One of the unique features of this group is the presence of sharp spurs on the legs of many of the males. One peacock-pheasant from Malaysia has as many as seven spurs on each leg! Spurs probably function primarily as weapons during fights between rival males, although this explanation is still rather controversial.

Most pheasants live in Asia or Africa, occupying a wide range of habitats from tropical rainforests to alpine grasslands. They tend to be fairly sedentary and use the same habitat throughout the year. Many of these hardy, adaptable birds have been introduced throughout the world as game birds.

Field Identification

The gaudy male ring-necked pheasant has a crimson face, metallic green head and neck, white collar, chestnut breast, and a long tapered tail. The female is a mottled mixture of brown, black, and tan. The hen is best identified by the length of her long tail.

Where to Find

No pheasant or partridge is native to North or South America, and both prairie species, the ring-necked pheasant and the gray partridge, were introduced by hunters in the 1800s. The ring-necked pheasant has prospered in its new home, and the bird is found throughout central North America. In the prairies, the pheasant favors croplands, weedy ditches, shelter-belts, and the shrubby areas along fence lines.

Wintering Grounds

On a sunny day, the sight of a flamboyantly feathered male pheasant running across the snow is enough color to overdose any photographer, and for 40 years I've been chasing that winter image. The pheasant stays on the prairies all winter. In late fall, neighboring birds usually band together, forming flocks of up to 50 individuals. The flocks disband and scatter at the start of the spring breeding season in April.

Diet and Feeding Habits

The ringed-necked pheasant is a scratch-and-peck feeder. It begins to forage within an hour of sunrise and can be seen moving about anytime during the day, which explains why they are seen so often in stubble fields. When grain is scarce, the birds eat weed seeds, berries, fresh green shoots, beetles, grasshoppers, crickets, and caterpillars.

Breeding Biology

The male pheasant begins to crow and flutter in early April, hoping to catch the ear of prospective mates. As many as 15 females may be lured to a "crowing area" and mate with the outspoken owner, although the average is only three or four. The male pheasant is extremely territorial and will chase and fight any rival male that dares to trespass. Although these battles are a wonderful blur of color to witness, they are a serious affair for the participants. Combatants tear at each other's wattles with their sharp-edged beaks and rake each other with their claws and spurs. Occasionally, one of the feathered warriors is killed.

Most hens lay their eggs within the crowing area of their mate. The nest is a shallow hollow on the ground, often hidden in the shrubbery or tall grasses of a roadside ditch. The female alone incubates the seven to fifteen eggs—the largest clutch of any prairie bird. The precocious chicks hatch after 25 to 27 days, and although they can feed themselves, the female still leads them to food, watches for danger, and broods them when they get cold. The young can fly by two weeks of age.

In some male pheasants the tail ❯ may comprise nearly half their total body length.

AMERICAN COOT *Fulica americana*

Family Details

Rail Family (Rallidae), 141 species worldwide, 4 prairie species

This large family includes the rails, coots, and gallinules. The behavior of these birds varies so drastically, it's surprising they are related. The rails represent one extreme. Many rails are solitary, secretive birds that skulk through dense marsh vegetation under the cover of darkness. They have narrow bodies that they can compress even further to squeeze through vegetation without noise or movement. These traits make rail-watching an exercise in frustration, and on most outings I hear the birds but never see them. For example, in prairie wetlands, I have heard the horse whinny call of the tiny sora hundreds of times, yet I have seen the bird fewer than a dozen times.

Coots and gallinules are at the other end of the behavior spectrum. These members of the Rail Family are active during the daytime, gregarious, and highly conspicuous, swimming and diving in open water.

One of the most interesting features of the Rail Family is that over 30 species of rails and gallinules living on islands are flightless, or nearly so. In every case, the islands lack predators. Birds, like all creatures, must balance the energy costs of their behavior with the benefits. Flying takes a great amount of energy, and flight muscles are a heavy burden to carry. On islands where rails no longer needed to escape from predators, it was advantageous for them to become flightless.

Field Identification

From a distance, the coot resembles a small, all-black duck with white feathers under its tail. Notice the chicken-like shape of its white beak and the way the bird bobs its head when it swims. "Mudhen" is one of the coot's nicknames. It also has a characteristic way of running across the water's surface for many meters, flapping its wings madly, before it finally becomes airborne.

Where to Find

The hardy, adaptable American coot is common and widespread on sloughs and lakes throughout the prairies.

Wintering Grounds

Prairie coots winter in the southern United States and Mexico. At this time of the year, they are highly gregarious and may gather in large noisy flocks containing up to 1,500 birds. Wintering coots can sometimes become "pests," and the surest way for them to do this is to irk a golfer. Coots love to graze on fairways and greens, and their bulky droppings can make putting a challenge. One year in California, tempers flared, and 400 coots were shot by employees of the golf course. More coots were back the next winter.

Diet and Feeding Habits

Coots are mainly vegetarians and eat the leaves, roots, and seeds of a great variety of aquatic plants. They dive to feed or upend

< *(left)* A coot's impressive claws are used as slashing weapons in fights between rivals. *(top)* The colorfulness of the ornamented head of a hatchling coot helps parents pick their favorites. (bottom) An adult will commonly dive and retrieve underwater vegetation to feed its young.

like a dabbling duck. They have long toes, fringed with lobes, and strong legs. A coot can stay underwater for 15 to 20 seconds and may reach depths of 7 meters (23 ft.). Besides aquatic plants they also eat insects, snails, and tadpoles. I have watched American widgeons, gadwalls, and northern shovelers loiter around a feeding coot and steal scraps of vegetation from it when it surfaces to swallow its meal.

Breeding Biology

The coot is a prairie bird with a self-important attitude. Pairs aggressively defend their nesting territory against any and all rivals. Intruders are quickly routed in a "splattering-attack" in which the attacker runs, flaps, and splashes noisily across the surface of the water. If the trespasser lingers and is caught by the owner, a fight may ensue. Fighting coots lean back on their tail, grab and slash with their long-clawed feet, pecking each other furiously with their beaks. Coots attack other birds as well, including every variety of prairie duck and grebe. They will even fearlessly chase and tackle a Canada goose that is five times heavier than a coot. One spring, my wife, Aubrey, and I spent several weeks photographing ducks from a blind. To our annoyance, the resident coots often drove away our subjects just as they swam within camera range. The standing joke became, Oh, oh, we're going to get "cooterized" again.

Courting male coots arch their wings above their back, flare the white feathers under their tail, and chase the female. The breeding pair builds up to nine floating platforms of cattails and aquatic plants, but they only use one as a nest for their eggs. The extra nests are used for preening, displays, copulation, and brooding their chicks. The average coot nest contains eight or nine speckled buffy eggs, and both sexes share in the 23- to 27-day incubation. Coot chicks leave the nest soon after hatching. They swim well and paddle along behind their parents, although they sometimes hitch a ride on an adult's back. The young can fly by six weeks of age.

→ **Trivia Tidbit**

In a long-term study, 40 percent of coot nests were parasitized by other coots and contained eggs laid by at least one foreign female. Astonishingly, male and female nest-owners recognize their own chicks and vigorously reject any parasitic chicks, pecking them and driving them away, even attempting to drown them. The foreign chicks that do escape eventually die. How do coots know which chicks are theirs? It seems coot parents recognize their own chicks by initially imprinting on cues given off by the first chick that hatches in the clutch, and they use these cues as a reference to discriminate against foreign chicks that usually hatch later. Chicks that do not match the imprinted cues are rejected and attacked, although the nature of these cues is unclear. Such behavior is only effective if the first egg to hatch always belongs to the nest-owners, and indeed it does in 90 percent of cases. Coots begin incubation before their entire clutch has been laid so the eggs do not hatch at the same time, and up to 10 days may separate the hatching of the first egg from that of the last. Parasitic females usually wait to sneak their eggs in after the nest-owner has already laid two or three eggs so a parasitic egg is rarely the first one to hatch.

‹ In a sustained "splatter-attack" by an irascible coot the chase can persist for 100 meters or more.

SANDHILL CRANE *Grus canadensis*

Family Details

Crane Family (Gruidae), 15 species worldwide, 2 prairie species

Cranes are large birds, all of whom are adapted for life around water and have long legs and necks. The family includes the tallest of all flying birds, the sarus crane of India and Australia, which is slightly taller than 1.5 meters (5 ft.), and about the height of my wife on a good hair day.

Cranes bugle and trumpet, producing some of the most delightful wild music in the natural world. The windpipe in most of these birds is exceptionally long and coils inside their breastbones. The long windpipe amplifies their calls, and many species can be heard several kilometers away.

Cranes are long-lived birds; some may live to 30 years of age. Generally, these birds mate for life. Their longevity, faithfulness, elegant stature, and elaborate courtship dances have elevated these majestic birds to symbols of good fortune in Asia. Nonetheless, 10 species are currently vulnerable or endangered, and one species, the Siberian crane, is critically endangered. Globally, the deterioration and loss of wetlands is the biggest threat currently facing cranes.

Field Identification

The sandhill crane is a tall gray bird with a featherless crimson crown and white cheeks. Juvenile birds are reddish brown in color but acquire adult plumage by the time they are one year old. Cranes fly with their long necks fully extended. Another large gray bird, the great blue heron, which may be mistaken for a sandhill, flies with its neck folded in an S-shape and its head nestled between its shoulders.

Where to Find

The sandhill formerly nested in the prairies. It now stops only to roost and feed in the area as it passes through on its annual spring and autumn migrations in April and September. Commonly, the birds roost in shallow open wetlands and feed in nearby stubble fields. In the autumn, large numbers of sandhills regularly stop at Last Mountain Lake, the Quill Lakes, and the Kindersley area of southern Saskatchewan as well as the Jasper-Pulaski Game Management Area in Indiana.

❮ The bare red skin on a crane's head intensifies in color when the bird gets excited.

(opposite) Cranes, Ross's geese and snow ❯ geese frequently overwinter in the same locations in the southern United States.

Wintering Grounds

Virtually all of the cranes migrating through the prairies winter in New Mexico and Texas. The birds migrate during the day, taking off a few hours after sunrise and landing one or two hours before sunset. Traveling in V-formation, and at speeds up to 80 kilometers per hour (50 mph) with a tailwind, they cover about 250 kilometers (155 mi.) a day. Young sandhills travel with their parents on their first migration. In cranes, unlike most birds, knowledge of migration routes and wintering sites is not instinctual and must be learned.

Diet and Feeding Habits

The crane is a big bird with a correspondingly big appetite that it satisfies by eating a great variety of foods. Its diet includes berries, waste grain, insects, birds' eggs, nestlings, frogs, snakes, and small mammals.

Breeding Biology

Adult sandhills usually do not breed until they are two or three years old, and some first-timers may be seven before they finally nest. Courtship begins on the wintering grounds and includes an elaborate "dance," in which partners repeatedly leap into the air with their wings outstretched, bugling in excitement.

Most of the cranes passing through the prairies are bound for muskeg bogs in the boreal forest or the soggy Arctic tundra. Sandhill eggs are olive-colored, splattered with dark brown and rusty blotches. The usual clutch of two is laid on a large mound of vegetation, a meter (3 ft.) or more across and 15 to 20 centimeters (6 to 8 in.) high. Both adults share in the month-long incubation of the eggs. Typically, egg number one hatches two to three days ahead of egg number two. By the time the second chick arrives, the older chick is much larger than the new arrival and a battle for survival begins.

The two chicks often fight and peck each other until one of them, usually the older one, drives away its sibling, which wanders off and eventually starves. Through all of this, the crane parents never intervene. The surviving chick stays with its parents until it is nine or 10 months old, about the time the adults migrate north again for the next breeding season.

→ **Trivia Tidbit**

The gray body plumage of the sandhill crane is often tinged with rust. The crane is one of the few birds in the world that actually "paints" its feathers. The crane purposefully dabs its plumage with wads of wet mud. Red iron pigments in the mud stain the bird's feathers a rusty color. The rusty staining makes the adult birds less conspicuous when they are sitting on their nests.

(top) The red staining on a crane's ❯ feathers results when the bird purposefully preens with mud rich in iron oxide. (left) Except during their summer breeding season, cranes migrate, forage, and roost in the safety of groups. *(right)* Typically, the eggs of the sandhill crane hatch two to three days apart.

WHOOPING CRANE *Grus americana*

Family Details

Crane Family (Gruidae), 15 species worldwide, 2 prairie species
See Sandhill Crane for a general discussion of the Crane Family.

Field Identification

The 1.2-meter (4-ft.) tall, all-white whooping crane is unmistakable when standing on the ground. In flight, it can be distinguished from a tundra swan by its black wingtips. Distinguishing it from a white pelican, which also has black wingtips, requires a closer look at the bird's head and neck. The crane has a very long outstretched neck whereas the pelican folds its neck back and flies with its head resting between its shoulders.

Where to Find

The endangered whooping crane narrowly escaped extinction in the 1940s when only 21 birds remained in the wilds of Canada's Wood Buffalo National Park. Today, the whooping crane is recognized by Canada's Species at Risk Registry as "a flagship species in North American wildlife conservation and symbolizes the struggle that characterizes many endangered species worldwide." Even so, despite

‹ When the U.S. Endangered Species
Act was passed in 1973 fewer than 50
whooping cranes remained in the wild.

nearly 80 years of intense protection and management by the United States and Canada, the wild population of these majestic cranes is still endangered and numbers less than 500 birds with an additional 160 birds in captivity.

Whooping cranes are seen regularly on migration in central Saskatchewan and occasionally in eastern Alberta. They routinely associate with sandhill cranes and can be sighted in the Last Mountain Lake area feeding in the surrounding croplands.

Wintering Grounds

After a two-day flight from their nesting grounds in Wood Buffalo National Park, family groups arrive in south-central Saskatchewan where they typically remain for up to five weeks feeding on waste grain in croplands. Afterward, they make a fast one-week flight across the U.S. prairie states to their main wintering grounds in the salt grass marshes and tidal flats of coastal Texas in and around Aransas National Wildlife Refuge.

The Wood Buffalo/Aransas population is currently the only self-sustaining population of whooping cranes. In the 1970s, biologists attempted to cross-foster whooping cranes with sandhill cranes in Idaho, but that plan failed. Afterward, an effort was made to establish a non-migratory population in central Florida. Over a 10-year period, roughly 300 captive-bred cranes were released in Florida. As of 2018, only 14 remained, and the survivors are scheduled to be relocated to southern Louisiana where the establishment of a new non-migratory population is being tried. Another ambitious reintroduction plan began in the early 2000s and relied on a human-piloted ultralight to guide captive-bred, imprinted cranes between Wisconsin and Florida. This population currently has about 100 birds in it, but this imaginative effort has now been discontinued because the hand-raised and guided birds have failed to reproduce in the wild.

Diet and Feeding Habits

On its northern breeding grounds the whooping crane is omnivorous. Typically, it probes in flooded and sandy soils for aquatic insects, crustaceans, minnows, frogs, and garter snakes. On the surface, it feeds on mice, voles, insects, berries, and seeds. In winter, the crane relies mostly on fiddler crabs, mud shrimp, crayfish, snails, and clams.

Breeding Biology

Whooping cranes begin to breed when they are three years old. Subadults associate on the wintering grounds, and, over one to three winters, eventually select a mate to breed exclusively with for multiple years. Their courtship behavior, which is often described as dancing, entails a combination of bowing, leaping, and flapping. Pairs return to their nesting areas in Wood Buffalo in late April. Nests are usually constructed in shallow water in marshes or along the edge of a lake and made from nearby bulrushes, sedges, and cattails heaped into a pile. A shallow depression on top holds the pair's one to two eggs, after which the 30-day incubation is shared by both partners. Though the pair may hatch two eggs, usually only a single chick survives. The parents stay with their chick for six to seven months with the family breaking up once it reaches its wintering grounds.

KILLDEER *Charadrius vociferus*

Family Details

Plover Family (Charadriidae), 66 species worldwide, 6 prairie species

This family includes the plovers and lapwings. It is the second-largest group of shorebirds after the curlews, sandpipers, snipes, and phalaropes. Unlike the curlew and sandpiper group, which displays a wide range of body sizes and beak shapes, the plovers are rather uniform in size and have a relatively short, blunt bill that is swollen near the tip.

The big-eyed plovers hunt by sight and pick their prey from the surface of the ground, unlike the sandpiper group, which probe the mud and "feel" for their food.

Many plovers have conspicuous black bands on their heads and breasts, and their plumage is often a bold mix of brown, olive, gray, black, and white, quite different from the plain, mottled-brown feathers so common among the snipes, curlews, and sandpipers. Even though plovers are boldly patterned, the black bands on their bodies break up their silhouette and help them blend in with their surroundings. Male and female plovers are similar in appearance.

Field Identification

The killdeer is roughly the size of a robin and is the most common plover on the prairies. The two black bands across the bird's white neck and breast distinguish it from all other species, and in flight, its rusty-colored rump is unmistakable. At close range, the killdeer has a narrow bright orange ring around its eyes.

The bird's common name is an imitation of its call, *kill-dee,*

kill-dee, and its scientific name, *vociferus*, reflects how loud and noisy it can be.

Where to Find
The killdeer is widespread throughout the prairies. As you might expect, the bird is a frequent visitor to sloughs, irrigation ponds, and wet pastures, but the adaptable plover is also common in cultivated fields, golf courses, airports, the gravel shoulders of roadways, and on dry prairies far from water. The killdeer was once the target of market hunters, but because of habitat changes caused by humans, it is arguably more common today than it ever was before.

Wintering Grounds
Killdeers overwinter in coastal regions from southern British Columbia all the way to northern South America. On their wintering grounds, the birds may forage alone or in loose flocks of up to 50 birds. The killdeer is often one of the earliest spring migrants to return to the prairies. In March, when snow patches still cover the ground, the bird's noisy calls are a welcome reminder that spring is on its way.

Diet and Feeding Habits
Throughout the year, the killdeer feeds primarily on insects and is especially skilled at capturing beetles and grasshoppers. The stomachs of some individuals may contain hundreds of weevils and grasshoppers, both of which are serious agricultural pests. The killdeer hunts in the usual plover manner of sprinting for a meter or two, freezing, then pecking the prey off the ground.

Breeding Biology
In the late 1950s, the bird-watching craze was still decades away. Then, as a 10-year-old boy, I liked to wander alone in the woods and fields of my uncle's dairy farm in southern Ontario and search for birds. A killdeer nest was the first bird's nest I ever found. I still remember my excitement at discovering the four speckled eggs resting in a hollow in the gravel at the edge of the road. When I accidentally flushed the adult bird from the nest, it flapped along the ground, dragging its wings, flaring its tail, and exposing its bright rusty rump. I thought for a moment that I had stepped on the bird and injured it. The killdeer, in common with many shorebirds, is an accomplished actor, and its "broken-wing display" is used to distract coyotes, foxes, and other predators and lure them away from its nest. Both the male and the female killdeer perform distraction displays, which tend to be most daring just before the eggs hatch at the end of the 25-day incubation period. The parents have invested a great amount of time and have the most to lose if the eggs are predated. Once the chicks hatch, they scatter and crouch in the grass whenever danger threatens. Young killdeers are less likely to be detected by a predator than are the eggs, so the parent birds take fewer risks to protect the chicks, and their distraction displays are less daring as time goes on. Hatchling killdeers forage with their parents until they begin to fly at around four weeks of age. After the first set of chicks are independent some adult killdeers may raise a second brood.

PIPING PLOVER *Charadrius melodus*

Family Details

Plover Family (Charadriidae), 66 species worldwide, 6 prairie species

See Killdeer for a general discussion of the Plover Family.

Field Identification

The piping plover is a small, pale shorebird with a white face, neck, and belly; sandy wings and back; and orange legs. The bird has a single black band across its forehead and another around its neck.

Where to Find

This attractive plover is the most endangered shorebird in North America. Two subspecies are recognized based on their geographic distribution. An eastern subspecies breeds along the Atlantic coast from Newfoundland to North Carolina, and an interior subspecies breeds primarily in the Great Plains from the Prairie Provinces south to Nebraska, with a few additional birds in the Great Lakes region of both Canada and the United States. The total piping plover population is thought to number around 8,000 birds. Just over 1,000 of these breed in the Canadian prairies, with the greatest number in Saskatchewan, where they nest along the shores of large alkaline lakes, such as Big Quill Lake and Chaplin Lake, and around Lake Diefenbaker.

Wintering Grounds

The piping plover overwinters on mudflats and sand beaches scattered along the Gulf of Mexico. One bird that was banded at Handhills Lake, Alberta, wintered three years in a row on Marco Island on the Gulf Coast of Florida. Most piping plovers leave the prairies by early August and return again in April.

Diet and Feeding Habits

The piping plover is closely tied to the shoreline, and generally feeds within five meters (16 ft.) of the water's edge. One North Dakota study revealed that the birds spent 42 percent of their time foraging at the waterline and 45 percent searching the gravel areas on the beach nearby.

The piping plover, as well as a number of other plovers, uses an intriguing feeding technique called "foot trembling." While standing still, the bird stretches a leg forward and rapidly stomps on the wet mud with its foot. Researchers believe this behavior may mimic the vibration of waves, fooling invertebrates buried in the mud into moving and exposing their location.

The plover eats any small invertebrate found on the beach: worms, midges, beetles, spiders, grasshoppers, and snails. At a lake in eastern Alberta, I watched fast-moving plovers run and snatch brine flies swarming along the water's edge. The birds fed alongside large flocks of migrating sanderlings and black-bellied plovers, all of whom were gorging on the abundance of insects.

Breeding Biology

Beginning in late April, male piping plovers each defend a small territory that includes a section of shoreline for foraging and an adjacent section of gravel beach for nesting. In a North Dakota study, the nests were sometimes as close as 14 meters (46 ft.) apart, but more often the distance was three times that. The plovers may use nothing more than a shallow scrape in the sand to cradle their four tan, speckled eggs. However, on gravel shorelines, the birds often line their nests with tiny pebbles and generally continue to add pebbles throughout laying and incubation.

The chicks hatch after 28 days, and, typical of all shorebirds, the downy youngsters can run, hide, and feed themselves within a day or two. Some adult females desert their brood after only five to 10 days, but in many cases both parents stay with the chicks even after they fledge and sometimes until the start of migration in August.

The prairie piping plover is in serious trouble for a number of reasons. When water levels drop in prairie lakes because of drought or excessive drainage for agriculture, grasses and other plants quickly invade the dry shorelines. When this happens, the shoreline is no longer suitable for nesting, and the plovers abandon the lake even if there is still an abundance of food.

Rising water levels in some lakes also pose a threat to nesting piping plovers. The best example of this is Lake Diefenbaker in southern Saskatchewan. This large reservoir once supported the highest number of piping plovers in Canada, perhaps 14 percent of the total population. Typically, the reservoir is filled in late May, just after the plovers have finished laying their eggs, and in some years many nests are lost to flooding.

Disturbance by livestock is yet another problem for plovers on the prairies. In one study in Saskatchewan, grazing cattle were identified as a major threat to the plovers on 21 lakes. Probably the number one cause of breeding failure in prairie plovers is predators. In various years predators have destroyed 40 percent of the plover nests in Manitoba, 72 percent in Saskatchewan, and 93 percent in North Dakota. The common culprits are red foxes, striped skunks, American crows, herring gulls, California gulls, and ring-billed gulls. In recent decades, these gulls have greatly increased in numbers, mainly because of their ability to scavenge off humans. More gulls has meant more pressure on nesting plovers. To counteract this threat, biologists in some areas now erect heavy fences over plover nests to protect them from predators as well as from trampling by cattle, and as a result hatching success has increased dramatically, sometimes exceeding 80 percent.

Despite the attention the piping plover has received, it is still too little, too late, and plover numbers continue to decline. Some authorities predict the bird may be gone from the prairies before the end of this century. That would be an embarrassing tragedy.

⟨ Many prairie mammals prey on the eggs and hatchlings of ground-nesting shorebirds. Predators include the red fox, American badger, coyote, mink, short-tailed weasel, and striped skunk.

BLACK-NECKED STILT *Himantopus mexicanus*

Family Details

The Stilt and Avocet Family (Recurvirostridae), 7 species world-wide, 2 prairie species

This is a small family of elegant, slim shorebirds whose bodies are slightly larger than that of a robin, but all have a long flexible neck and especially long legs. For its size, the black-necked stilt of the prairies has the longest legs of any bird in North America. The literal translation of the scientific name for the family, Recurvirostridae, means "backward curving bill." The stilts have a slightly upturned bill and that of the avocets is strongly upturned. The stilts and avocets, unlike most shore-birds, nest in loose colonies, and the birds tend to be even more gregarious outside the breeding season. In winter, flocks of several thousand birds may feed together.

Field Identification

The handsome long-necked stilt is easy to recognize with its stark black-and-white plumage. The bird has a long, slender black bill and very long red legs. At close range, it is possible to see a brownish tinge on the feathers of the female's back; otherwise the sexes are indistinguishable.

‹ Brown back feathers readily identify this stilt as a female.

Where to Find

Until 35 years ago, the black-necked stilt was listed as an erratic visitor and very rare breeder in prairie Alberta. Two nests found in 1977 were attributed to drought conditions, which presumably encouraged the birds to nest farther north than usual. In the spring of 1998—a warm, dry El Nino year—hundreds of stilts were seen in southern Alberta and dozens of nests were reported. Since that time, stilt numbers have slowly increased, and the bird is now a relatively common breeder in the shallow alkaline sloughs of the southern third of the province. Breeding stilts are now also found in the prairies of Saskatchewan and Manitoba. The stilt often associates with its close relative, the American avocet.

Wintering Grounds

Black-necked stilts winter along the southern coast of California and on shallow mudflats along both coasts of Mexico. Migrants fly south from the prairies in August and September.

Diet and Feeding Habits

The stilt eats mosquito larvae, diving beetles, caddisflies, mayfly and dragonfly nymphs, grasshoppers, snails, and tiny fish. The bird has unusually strong jaw muscles, and this enables it to rapidly close its beak and get a firm grasp on small prey. Typically, the

black-necked stilt feeds in shallow water where its breast feathers can stay dry, picking food from the surface and the upper few centimeters of the water column. The stilt and the avocet share the same diet, and the two lessen competition somewhat by simply concentrating on slightly different water depths, the stilt on the surface and the avocet deeper down.

Breeding Biology

The black-necked stilt usually returns to the Canadian prairies in mid-April, and by the end of the month some pairs are already mating. Stilts nest in small colonies on the ground and usually build simple mounds of grass stems and twigs hidden in sedges or other short marsh vegetation in shallow water.

The stilt usually lays a clutch of four pale brownish, cryptic eggs covered with dark spots and blotches. Both sexes share the 24-day incubation. In hot weather, an incubating pair might make more than 100 daily trips to soak their belly feathers in water in order to cool the eggs. New hatchlings look like tiny clumps of down balanced on a pair of toothpicks. Young stilts can run and feed themselves almost from the moment they hatch, but they follow their parents around for about a month, until they begin to fly.

‹ *(top)* The female stilt on the right is thrashing the water in a courtship display soliciting copulation. *(bottom)* A stilt's nest needs to be high enough above the water to prevent lethal flooding of the eggs.

The mating sequence of the avocet starts ❯
with solicitation, followed by mounting,
and concludes with a stylized beak
display and a celebratory march.

AMERICAN AVOCET *Recurvirostra americana*

Family Details

The Stilt and Avocet Family (Recurvirostridae), 7 species world-wide, 2 prairie species

See Black-necked Stilt for a general discussion of the Stilt and Avocet Family.

Field Identification

The avocet is a strikingly beautiful shorebird. It has a black-and-white body, rusty head and neck, and long bluish gray legs. The female's bill is noticeably shorter and more upturned than that of the male; otherwise the sexes are identical.

Where to Find

The American avocet is widespread and common on shallow sloughs and marshes throughout the prairies. The bird is often associated with alkaline wetlands and the mudflats of shallow lakes and irrigation ponds.

Wintering Grounds

Most avocets spend the winter on intertidal mudflats, brackish-water ponds, and impoundments along the Pacific or Atlantic coasts of Mexico and Central America. Like most shorebirds, they migrate south before the end of summer, with the peak exodus occurring in late August.

Diet and Feeding Habits

The inside of an avocet's bill is fringed, and the bird uses this to filter minute food items from the water. The most common foods include snails, aquatic beetles, dragonfly nymphs, water boatmen, midges, and water fleas, but they also eat some seeds and small bits of water plants. In alkaline sloughs, avocets eat large numbers of brine shrimp and brine flies. The classic way for an avocet to feed is to sweep its bill back and forth through the water, wielding its beak as if it were a scythe. The birds also pick food off the surface and submerge their heads to capture underwater prey.

Breeding Biology

Avocets usually form pairs on their wintering grounds or during their spring migration. Soon after they return to the prairies in late April, the pairs stake out and defend small feeding territories. These territories may or may not be close to their eventual nest site. Both the male and the female will aggressively drive away rival avocets.

Avocets nest in small loose colonies along shorelines or on islands, which afford them some protection from coyotes, foxes, and skunks. In early May 2019, I spent dozens of hours watching avocets. I saw their elaborate mating ritual many times. I described it in my journal: "It is early evening and a pair of avocets is very close to my blind, their elegant bodies perfectly reflected in the smooth blue water of the slough. Suddenly the female bows forward and stretches her neck low down, just above the surface of the water. She stays frozen in this pose. I can tell it is the female by the greater curve in her beak. Her mate begins to preen vigorously, dipping his bill in the water and splashing the female in the process. The male walks excitedly from one side of the female to the other, the intensity of his preening and water splashing increasing with every moment. After eight or nine changes in position, the male jumps onto the female's back, fluttering his wings to keep his balance. For an instant their cloacas 'kiss,' then the male slides off and the pair run together through the water for a dozen steps, their bills crossed like the swords of two fencers."

Avocets build a simple nest of grass and twigs on the ground. I have found many nests, and they were always in the open. The cryptically colored, pear-shaped eggs, usually four of them, blend well with the surroundings and make the nest very difficult to locate. Both sexes take turns incubating the eggs for the 23-day period. The birds alternate frequently throughout the day, changing places every 40 to 80 minutes. In hot weather, the incubating parents soak their belly feathers in water before sitting on the nest. This cools the eggs and keeps the nest humidity high. The chicks are able to leave the nest within two hours of hatching, and they stay with their parents until they are four weeks old and have begun to fly.

LONG-BILLED CURLEW *Numenius americanus*

Family Details

Curlew, Sandpiper, Snipe, and Phalarope Family (Scolopacidae), 92 species worldwide, 20 prairie species

The common name for this family of small- to medium-sized birds is shorebirds. Although all of them swim well and walk and run with ease on dry land, they are best known for their habit of wading and feeding in shallow water along beaches and coastlines. Most of the family members are rather plainly colored in buff, grays, and browns, but they vary greatly in size from the sparrow-sized sandpipers, called "peeps," to the large crow-sized godwits and curlews. With the exception of the phalaropes, male and female birds in this family are quite similar in appearance

Shorebirds display a great variety of bill sizes and shapes. This diversity enables them to exploit a wider range of foods and lessens the competition between them. Within the family, there are sandpipers with slender pointed bills that rapidly probe the mud like the needle on a sewing machine, needle-nosed phalaropes that deftly pick minute plankton from the water's surface, flat-beaked turnstones that flip over pebbles to uncover hidden prey, godwits with long upturned bills, and curlews with bills that curve downward. Most of these birds have bill tips that are densely covered with sensitive touch receptors that allow the owner to detect food buried deep in the mud. Through a remarkable feat of engineering, a shorebird is able to open just the tip of its bill while the rest remains closed. The bone inside the upper part of the beak slides forward, causing the tip to bend upward. The bird then pinches the prey in the movable tip and out it comes.

Field Identification

The crow-sized long-billed curlew has a wingspan up to 100 centimeters (39 in.), making it the largest shorebird in North America. The curlew is mottled brown in color, but in flight its cinnamon-colored "armpits" are clearly visible and distinguish it from all other large shorebirds. As its name suggests, the bird's 23-centimeter (9-in.) long curved bill is its most distinctive feature.

Female curlews are larger than their mates and have an appreciably longer bill. The typical call of the curlew is a loud, plaintive cur-lew, usually repeated.

Where to Find

The curlew is an uncommon resident of the dry short-grass prairies. In Canada, the species has been slowly declining over the last 50 years and is currently listed as a species of special concern. The fragmentation and loss of habitat to cultivation and urban development as well as climate change are the main reasons for its decline.

Wintering Grounds

The long-billed curlew winters on mudflats and beaches from California and Texas south to Guatemala. The birds migrate south in August and return to the prairies in early April.

Diet and Feeding Habits

A foraging long-billed curlew seems very much out of place as it walks purposefully across the dry prairies, pecking here and there for grasshoppers, crickets, caterpillars, and nestling songbirds. A feeding bird is in constant motion as it zigzags across the prairie, wielding its extraordinary bill more deftly than a surgeon with a long-handled pair of forceps. On the wintering grounds, the curlew uses its long bill to probe tidal flats for lugworms, rag worms, and clams buried deep in the mud.

Breeding Biology

An adult long-billed curlew may not begin to breed until it is three years old. Often, birds are already paired when they arrive on the breeding grounds. Unpaired males immediately begin to perform conspicuous gliding displays, floating over the flat prairies, calling loudly to advertise their availability as well as their vigor and health.

When an incubating curlew becomes > overheated it flutters its throat to cool itself.

Curlews, in common with all shorebirds, lay four pear-shaped eggs that fit perfectly together. The nest consists of a shallow scrape on the ground scantily lined with fine grasses. Even with the nest being out in the open prairie, the heavily speckled, buff-colored eggs are very hard to see. The cryptic coloration of the adults also makes the nest very difficult for predators to locate. I once slowly crawled within a few meters of an incubating curlew to examine the fine pattern and color of its plumage. There is nothing quite as exciting as being within a few arm's lengths of a wild creature, with the soft wind of the prairie stroking your cheek and the fragrant aroma of grass and sun-heated sage filling your nostrils. The curlew stayed perfectly still, its neck stretched along the ground, and it remained that way as I slowly backed away, my heart pounding with excitement.

Both sexes incubate the eggs until they hatch at 28 days. Commonly, the eggs hatch within five hours of each other, and the downy chicks leave the nest within a day. From the beginning, young curlew chicks feed themselves, but they are brooded by both parents whenever they become cold or bad weather threatens. The female usually abandons her brood when they are just two to three weeks old, and the male continues to guard them until they fledge, at six weeks of age.

(opposite) Curlew chicks hatch ❯ synchronously, usually within four to six hours of each other. They quickly abandon the family nest, sometimes even before their down is dry.

The long-billed curlew, as is typical of ❯ most shorebirds, lays a clutch of four cryptic pyriform eggs.

WILLET *Catoptrophorus semipalmatus*

Family Details

Curlew, Sandpiper, Snipe, and Phalarope Family (Scolopacidae), 92 species worldwide, 20 prairie species

See Long-billed Curlew for a general discussion of the Curlew, Sandpiper, Snipe, and Phalarope Family.

Field Identification

The willet is a grayish, medium-sized sandpiper that is rather plain looking when it is loafing on the shoreline or wading in the shallows. In flight, however, the bird flaunts its white rump and striking black-and-white wings. The unmistakable "flashing" wing pattern is visible from a great distance and undoubtedly functions as a signal for other birds.

Where to Find

The willet is one of the most common shorebirds in the prairies. This unwary, noisy sandpiper frequents sloughs, irrigation ponds, wet meadows, and ditches. Sometimes, the first clue to the willet's presence is the distinctive sound of its loud call, in which it repeatedly sings its name.

(top) The black pigment melanin ❯ strengthens feathers against abrasion and is a common wingtip coloration in many birds. *(bottom)* When foraging, a willet will sometimes dip its head underwater but more often limits itself to the shallow surface layers of the slough.

Wintering Grounds

Willets spend the winter along the southern Pacific and Atlantic coasts of the United States. I have photographed these birds on the muddy tidal flats of southern Florida. When a whole flock takes flight their flashing black-and-white wings produce a dazzling effect.

Diet and Feeding Habits

The willet has a stout beak for its size, and it eats the larger aquatic invertebrates that lurk in the mud and water of the slough: worms, snails, beetles, dragonfly nymphs, small fish, and leeches. One spring, I was surprised when a willet grabbed a large predatory water beetle that seemed to be half the size of the bird's head. The beetle was gone in a gulp.

Breeding Biology

Willets are highly aggressive birds, and the males defend their territory with a conspicuous flight display during which they fly in circles with their wings arched downward, flapping them in short rapid beats. The wing action creates a flickering pattern. Some males climb so high they are almost out of sight.

Willet nests are well hidden in heavy grasses and are generally located near water. On occasion, I have found some of their nests far out on the dry prairie with no water in sight. The birds normally lay four eggs, with the female doing most of the incubation, though the male may take over at night. The precocious chicks leave the nest as soon as they hatch. In late spring, when temperatures can be cool, young downy willets scurry around the prairie pecking and probing until they slowly become chilled. Their movements gradually slow down as their body temperature drops from its normal 40°C (104°F) to 31°C or 32°C (88 to 90°F). When this happens, they huddle under a parent, quickly warm up, and off they go again. Author Dr. Paul Johnsgard reported in *The Plovers, Sandpipers, and Snipes of the World* that an adult willet carried each of its four newly hatched chicks between its thighs across several creeks and over a marshland for a distance of half a kilometer (0.3 mi.).

The female adult abandons her chicks after several weeks, leaving the male to care for the young. The male may also abandon the chicks before they fledge, but this aspect of the willet's life has not been well studied.

The willet's loud ringing call, *pill-will-willet, pill-will-willet, pill-will-willet*, is the origin of the bird's common name.

UPLAND SANDPIPER *Bartramia longcauda*

Family Details

Curlew, Sandpiper, Snipe, and Phalarope Family (Scolopacidae), 92 species worldwide, 20 prairie species

See Long-billed Curlew for a general discussion of the Curlew, Sandpiper, Snipe, and Phalarope Family.

Field Identification

The upland sandpiper has a relatively small head, large eyes, a long neck and tail, and bright yellow legs and beak. This medium-sized sandpiper often lands on fence posts, telephone poles, and large boulders. When it alights, it frequently holds its wings extended above its back for a moment or two before folding them.

Where to Find

At the turn of the century, the upland sandpiper was much more widespread than it is today and was one of the most common birds on the prairies. Today, this pretty sandpiper occurs in localized patches throughout the prairies wherever native grasslands have been spared from the plow. The upland sandpiper, unlike most prairie shorebirds, is rarely found near water. As its name suggests, the bird prefers pastures, rangelands, and dry rolling prairies.

‹ *(left)* The upland sandpiper frequently lands on fenceposts, an elevated perch from which it can scan the surrounding prairie for intruders. *(right)* The upland sandpiper is an atypical-looking shorebird with its long neck and small dove-like head.

Wintering Grounds

The upland sandpiper, like so many shorebirds, is a long-distance migrant that flees to the warmer climes of South America in late summer, well before the first icy winds of autumn sweep down across the prairies. Most of these birds winter in the grasslands of southern Brazil and in northern and central Argentina. By April, these delightful songsters are back again enlivening the skies over native grasslands.

Diet and Feeding Habits

The upland sandpiper is a sprint-and-peck predator, dashing here and there to catch grasshoppers, weevils, and crickets. It also eats caterpillars, beetles, ants, moths, flies, spiders, snails, bugs, centipedes, millipedes, and earthworms—essentially anything that wiggles, creeps, scuttles, and flutters.

Breeding Biology

The male upland sandpiper, in common with many different birds living on the flat treeless prairies, sings on the wing while circling high in the sky. The bird's drawn out whistle reminds me of the "wolf" whistle my friends and I used as teenagers when we wanted to flirt with a girl. The whistle is more effective for the male sandpiper than it was for me.

Most sandpipers are already paired when they return to the prairies in spring, and the partners quickly claim a territory and whistle the news to the neighbors. Within two weeks of arrival, most of the pairs have begun to nest. In a North Dakota study, 183 out of 199 nests were located in native prairie. Some prairie shorebirds, such as curlews, willets, and godwits, have adapted somewhat to agricultural land and sometimes nest in stubble fields; the upland sandpiper never has and when the native prairie disappears, so will it.

A tuft of overhanging grass often hides the sandpiper's nest, which is usually a simple hollow on the ground lined with small twigs, leaves, and grasses. The usual clutch of four glossy, speckled eggs is incubated for three weeks, the duties shared by both partners. Within a day of hatching, young sandpiper chicks leave the nest and follow their parents, who continue to brood them and alert them to danger for a month afterward.

→ **Trivia Tidbit**

In the 1880s, when passenger pigeon numbers began to decline from overhunting, the market gunners shifted their sights to upland sandpipers. Great numbers of these prairie birds were slaughtered during their spring migration when they passed overhead in enormous flocks. Eventually, the hunting stopped, and the sandpipers began a slow recovery but never regained their former abundance. Today, the steady loss of native grasslands threatens to reduce their numbers once again. In prairie Canada, the upland sandpiper has been declining by 2 percent every year for the last 30 years.

MARBLED GODWIT *Limosa fedoa*

Family Details

Curlew, Sandpiper, Snipe, and Phalarope Family (Scolopacidae), 92 species worldwide, 20 prairie species

See Long-billed Curlew for a general discussion of the Curlew, Sandpiper, Snipe, and Phalarope Family.

Field Identification

The marbled godwit, with a wingspan of 80 centimeters (32 in.), is one of the largest prairie shorebirds, second only in size to the long-billed curlew. The godwit is mottled brown in color with conspicuous cinnamon linings on the undersides of its wings. The bird has a long, upturned bill with an orange base that distinguishes it from the curlew, whose bill curves strongly downward.

Where to Find

The godwit is a bird of the northern Great Plains, being found in short-grass prairies, flooded fields, alkaline lakes, and sloughs. In the best wetland habitats, there may be three pairs of nesting godwits per square kilometer (0.4 sq. mi.).

Wintering Grounds

Most marbled godwits winter on the mud flats, beaches, and associated wetlands of the southern Pacific and Atlantic coasts of the United States. A few birds may migrate as far as Central America.

Diet and Feeding Habits

When the godwit feeds on dry uplands, it concentrates on grasshoppers and beetles, probing tufts of vegetation for insects hidden in the greenery. In water, the bird wades to the top of its thighs and often submerges its head to probe deeply into the mud with its 13-centimeter (5-in.) long bill. The godwit "feels" for leeches, worms, and insect larvae using the rich network of sensors at the tip of its beak. Because it does not use vision to locate most of its food, the godwit can also feed at night.

Breeding Biology

The marbled godwit returns to the prairies in early May. I have often watched energetic male godwits perform their aerial display, called a "ceremonial flight," over the edge of the slough. I described one such performance in my journal.

This is the fourth day in a row that I have watched the godwit wheel and sing over the prairie. The bird usually climbs to an altitude of about 50 meters (164 ft.) and slowly circles while calling loudly. The rich cinnamon of his underwings flashes brightly in the warmth of the late afternoon sun. At the end of his circular glide, he sometimes folds his wings and plummets toward the ground in a power dive, only to brake at the last moment and land softly. In a final display, the grounded godwit momentarily holds his rusty wings aloft as if he were saluting his own aerial achievement. His mastery of flight is a delight to watch.

The godwit usually nests on the ground on the open prairie, sometimes quite far from water. It may also nest in small, loose colonies, with three or four nests clustered within several hundred square meters. The birds lay four glossy, olive-brown eggs patterned with scrawls and small blotches. Both parents share the three-week incubation and afterward stay with the chicks for up to a month until they finally fledge.

‹ *(left)* The cinnamon-colored underwings on the godwit are clearly visible in flight and a good field sign to identify the bird. *(right)* These male godwits fought for over 11 minutes, after which the winner flew off with the female who was nearby watching the spectacle.

The generic name for the godwit, › Limosa, is Latin for muddy, a reflection of the muddy estuaries where the birds commonly forage in winter.

COMMON SNIPE *Gallinago gallinago*

Family Details

Curlew, Sandpiper, Snipe, and Phalarope Family (Scolopacidae), 92 species worldwide, 20 prairie species

See Long-billed Curlew for a general discussion of the Curlew, Sandpiper, Snipe, and Phalarope Family.

Field Identification

The snipe is a stocky shorebird with a boldly striped back, long beak, short legs, and short wings. Its bill length distinguishes it from all other prairie breeding shorebirds of similar size. The snipe is most often encountered when it suddenly flushes from marshy grasses, flying away in a rapid, zigzag course while emitting a hoarse, raspy call.

Where to Find

During the spring breeding season the common snipe often perches on roadside fence posts adjacent to flooded ditches. At other times, it frequents wet pastures, flooded fallow fields, and the marshy edges of sloughs and creeks. The secretive snipe prefers short vegetation that offers concealment but also provides a good view of approaching predators. These birds generally avoid tall dense vegetation, such as cattails and bulrushes.

Wintering Grounds

Snipes like to migrate on moonlit nights, often in flocks whose contact calls are audible from the ground. The chunky birds begin their southbound migration in August with many wintering in the southern United States or Mexico, while some fly as far as Venezuela. They return to the northern prairies in April.

Diet and Feeding Habits

The snipe commonly probes waterlogged soils with its long sensitive bill, searching for invertebrates, especially juicy earthworms. While foraging, it may immerse its entire beak and head. Smaller prey is often swallowed underwater, and researchers believe the birds obtain food by sucking it up from the soil. The snipe has backward-facing spicules inside its bill that prevent slippery food from escaping. A quarter of a snipe's stomach may consist of mud and grit, which help the bird to periodically regurgitate pellets of indigestible plant and insect parts.

Breeding Biology

One of the great delights of the common snipe is the male's spring aerial display called winnowing—a tremulous who-who-who-who produced when air flows rapidly over the bird's outstretched tail feathers causing them to vibrate audibly. The sound is produced during a high-speed dive, sometimes from as high as 600 meters (1,970 ft.). The displaying bird can be hard to locate because of its small size and the display height. An energetic male may winnow continuously for up to an hour, warning rival males against trespassing, and hoping to attract a potential female partner.

The monogamous pair builds a well-concealed nest, commonly on a grassy hummock, close to water or even surrounded by it. The four cryptic eggs are incubated for 18 to 20 days primarily by the female. The eggs hatch within three to four hours of each other, and the downy chicks leave the nest soon afterward. The first two chicks to hatch are led away from the nest by the male, and the female follows later with the remaining two. Typically, after abandoning the nest, the mates and their chicks have no contact with each other.

Snipe parents feed their chicks bill to bill, but the young begin to peck and probe for their own food within six days and are able to feed themselves completely by about 10 days of age. They may continue to beg for food from their parents until they are two months old, when they finally become independent.

The eyes of a snipe are set so far ›
back on its head that its field
of vision is almost 360 degrees.

WILSON'S PHALAROPE *Phalaropus tricolor*

Family Details

Curlew, Sandpiper, Snipe, and Phalarope Family (Scolopacidae), 92 species worldwide, 20 prairie species

See Long-billed Curlew for a general discussion of the Curlew, Sandpiper, Snipe, and Phalarope Family.

Field Identification

Wilson's phalarope is a small shorebird with a needle-like beak. The bird feeds on the water's surface and often spins like a top. The female phalarope is larger and more brightly colored than the male. She has a bold black stripe on the side of her face and neck, rust and gray back and wings, and a white belly. The male is similarly patterned but duller in tone.

Where to Find

The phalarope is found throughout the prairies in soggy ditches, shallow sloughs, and sedge wetlands.

(opposite) Both of these pale-colored ❯ male phalaropes were following the same solitary richly colored female for considerable time until one of them finally attacked and drove his rival away.

Wintering Grounds

The phalarope is one of the few shorebirds that migrates to an area specifically to molt at the end of the breeding season. Females begin to leave the prairie breeding areas as early as mid-June. The males follow several weeks later, and juveniles are the last to leave. They all gather on large alkaline lakes, such as Old Wives Lake and Chaplin Lake in Saskatchewan, Lake Abert in Oregon, and Mono Lake in California. Over 600,000 Wilson's phalaropes may gather at the Great Salt Lake in Utah. In these alkaline lakes, the birds molt and fatten in preparation for the rigors of their long southward migration. The autumn migration begins in late July and occurs throughout August. Most Wilson's phalaropes fly to alkaline lakes in the high Andes of Bolivia, Argentina, and Chile. They make this exhausting 5,500-kilometer (3,400-mi.) journey in a single, nonstop flight lasting 54 hours or more.

Diet and Feeding Habits

Phalaropes eat all the usual small aquatic invertebrates: beetles, fly larvae, snails, water boatmen, and damselfly nymphs. On alkaline lakes, they commonly gorge on brine shrimp and brine flies until their bodies are padded in fat. The phalarope often uses a distinctive feeding technique called spinning. Like a whirling dervish, a hungry phalarope spins rapidly around in a tight circle on the surface of the water. The spinning produces a miniature whirlpool that funnels insects and small aquatic invertebrates toward the surface, where they are stabbed by the pirouetting predator.

Phalaropes may also follow wading avocets to feed on any tiny animals that are stirred up by the birds' feet. In the High Andes of northern Chile, at an altitude of 4,400 meters (14,400 ft.), I watched phalaropes follow Andean and James flamingos for exactly the same reason.

Breeding Biology

In general, shorebirds show the greatest variety of mating systems of any group of birds. Some species are monogamous, many are promiscuous. In some cases, males breed in sequence or simultaneously with several females in a single season; in other instances, the female raises several families, each fathered by a different male. The phalaropes, however, carry the avian sexual revolution one step further: in these birds, the sexes have completely reversed their roles. Female Wilson's phalaropes are more brightly colored and larger than the males. Up to 10 aggressive females may court and follow a single harried male in an aerial chase. To win a mate, the females may even fight each other with flapping wings and stabbing beaks. A successful female "jealously" guards her partner. Under her watchful eye, the male builds a nest of fine grasses on the ground, and once the eggs are laid, he alone incubates them. The female phalarope deserts her partner soon after he begins to incubate. She may then try to mate with a second partner or simply migrate to a molting area. Meanwhile, the male phalarope incubates the eggs for about three weeks and stays with the chicks for another three weeks afterward. During this time he leads them from one feeding area to the next, broods them when it is cold, and warns them when a predator appears.

The successful male from the fight on the previous page quickly claimed his prize and mated with the female. The plumage differences between the sexes are clearly visible.

CALIFORNIA GULL *Larus californicus*

Family Details

Gull and Tern Family (Laridae), 97 species worldwide, 7 prairie species

The familiar gulls are a family of heavy-bodied, medium-sized to large seabirds. All have long, narrow pointed wings, webbed feet, and a stout hooked bill. The adaptable gulls will eat almost anything they can swallow, and many are accomplished scavengers. This flexibility has enabled the family to inhabit every continent, and to occupy a greater range of latitudes (84°North to 68°South) than any other group of birds on Earth.

Gulls are seabirds, and most species are found primarily in coastal regions. In North America, however, some species occur far inland. The three gulls in the prairies are good examples of this, and all have large breeding ranges in the center of the continent.

Terns, like gulls, are a group of seabirds that often range inland, far from the ocean. They are generally smaller than gulls and are more slender and graceful. Most have long, narrow, pointed wings

A prairie nesting colony of California gulls ❯ may contain hundreds of pairs. Where possible, an island is the preferred site because of a lower risk from mammalian predators, especially coyotes.

and a forked tail. Many terns can hover in one spot and dive from the air to capture small fish and aquatic insects.

Terns fly in a light, buoyant manner, yet this relaxed flight can carry some of them literally to the ends of the Earth. Many Arctic terns, for example, nest on the Arctic tundra in summer and overwinter in the pack ice of the Antarctic. To accomplish this, the bird makes an annual round-trip flight of up to 50,000 kilometers (30,000 mi.), the longest migration of any creature on the planet.

Field Identification

The California gull is a medium-sized gull with a white head and neck, gray back, gray wings with black wingtips, and yellow legs. It differs from the ring-billed gull by having dark brown eyes, and its yellow bill has red and black spots on the tip. Adult male and female Californias, as in all gulls, are similar in appearance.

It takes four years for a California gull to acquire its full adult appearance, and therefore a young gull can be a huge challenge to identify. In its first summer, a juvenile is all brown with black legs and a pink bill tipped with black. As it ages, the color of its legs changes from black to pink, to gray, and finally yellow. As

well, white feathers gradually appear in the plumage, giving the bird a mottled appearance until eventually it turns a solid white and gray.

Where to Find

The breeding range of the California gull is concentrated in the northern Great Plains where there are roughly 200 colonies of these gregarious seabirds. Alberta has the greatest number of colonies, with 50, six of which contain over 20,000 birds each. Saskatchewan ranks second, with 21 colonies. Both Montana and Utah have 19 colonies. Throughout their range the gulls frequent large sloughs, lakes, reservoirs, farmlands, and garbage dumps.

Wintering Grounds

Most California gulls winter along the Pacific Coast from Washington State to central Mexico. The birds are unusual because they continually change locations throughout the autumn, winter, and spring. Rather than restricting themselves to a single wintering site, the gulls slowly wander over a huge wintering range.

A clutch of four eggs is unusual ❯
in California gulls and more often
results from two females laying
eggs in the same nest.

Diet and Feeding Habits

The California gull, like many other gulls, is very resourceful at finding food. In irrigated fields, it waits for voles and pocket gophers to get flooded out of their burrows. The gulls also follow plows to feed on exposed insects and earthworms, and in croplands they feed on great numbers of grasshoppers. The birds' prodigious appetite for grasshoppers earned them a large gilded statue erected by early Mormons in Salt Lake City, Utah, to commemorate the gull's role in ridding crops of these plant-munching insects.

California gulls often share nesting islands with ring-billed gulls and double-crested cormorants, and they readily gobble up any unattended eggs and small chicks belonging to these species. Californias will also cannibalize their own kind and eat the eggs and chicks of any inattentive neighbors. In fact, chicks up to 40 days old are very vulnerable and may be attacked and killed anytime they wander out of their parents' protective territory.

Breeding Biology

California gulls often return to the prairies by the end of March. One year, I hiked out to an island colony in a slough that still had 20 centimeters (8 in.) of ice on it. The island was covered with snow, and the gulls had already begun setting up their nesting territories.

The gulls lay two to three blotched olive-green eggs in a simple ground nest made of dried grasses, discarded feathers, and dried bird bones left from previous nesting seasons. Gull pairs build their nest together, and both sexes incubate the eggs, taking shifts of three to four hours, which gives the off-duty bird enough time to forage. The downy, salt-and-pepper patterned chicks are fed regurgitated food by both adults until they fledge at about six weeks of age.

< If a gull pair successfully raises chicks the couple may remain together in succeeding seasons, but more often they pair with a different partner every year.

The conspicuous red dot near the tip > of the gull's beak is called a releaser spot. If a hungry chick pecks this spot it stimulates its parent to regurgitate food in response.

RING-BILLED GULL *Larus delawarensis*

Family Details

Gull and Tern Family (Laridae), 97 species worldwide, 7 prairie species

See California Gull for a general discussion of the Gull and Tern Family.

Field Identification

The ring-billed gull is smaller than the California gull but very similar in appearance. Both have white heads and black wingtips and from a distance may be difficult to distinguish. If you get close enough you will notice the ring-billed gull has pale yellow eyes and its bright yellow bill has a black band near the tip.

Ring-bills take three years to acquire their full adult appearance. The juveniles are mottled brown with dark eyes, a dark beak, and gray legs. As they mature, their eyes, beak, and legs lighten in color, the mottling gradually disappears, and their dark feathers are replaced with white and gray ones.

Where to Find

The ring-billed gull is widespread and common throughout the prairies and is found in sloughs, cultivated fields, and irrigated croplands.

Wintering Grounds

The ring-bill winters in the southern United States on inland lakes and waterways and along the coasts. This gull is extremely gregarious; as many as 50,000 birds may gather at a single landfill. The gulls migrate south in October and are among the last birds to leave the prairies in autumn. They migrate north again in early April.

Diet and Feeding Habits

The ring-bill frequently forages in fields, especially in the spring after the land has been freshly plowed. Its most important food are earthworms, but they also eat insects, meadow voles, deer mice, and waste grain. One of its favorite hangouts is the parking lot of fast-food restaurants, where it scavenges garbage and begs for food scraps. When I see these birds scrounging around my favorite hamburger outlets, I am reassured that the food is at least marginally edible. Having said that, ring-bills seem to have an iron-coated digestive tract and perhaps I should re-evaluate them as food critics.

Breeding Biology

These birds are just as gregarious on their breeding grounds as they are on their wintering grounds. In the prairies, hundreds and even thousands of birds may gather at a single nesting colony. In the east, around the Great Lakes, there are immense ring-bill colonies, some containing up to 80,000 nesting pairs! Most colonies are located on islands, which greatly lessens the risk from egg-napping coyotes, red foxes, and striped skunks. A marauding skunk, for example, may destroy 30 to 40 nests in a single nighttime raid. The total damage, however, may be much greater than this since

many eggs are broken when the startled gulls fly off in panic. As well, other eggs are lost when they become excessively cooled because the frightened adults delay returning to their nests.

Ring-bills lay one to three olive-gray eggs that are heavily marked with dark splotches. The nest is a sparse collection of twigs, small sticks, grasses, and leaves piled on the ground. Both sexes build the nest and share in the incubation duties. Dense colonies may have two or three nests in every square meter (9 sq. ft.), and the neighbors bicker continuously. If an egg accidentally rolls out of the nest during an argument, the owner will retrieve it. This behavior is instinctive, and sometimes the birds get their wires crossed. In one Oregon colony, 4 percent of the nests contained egg-sized pebbles, which the gulls probably mistook for errant eggs.

Nestling gull chicks are covered with down, their eyes are open, and they can walk around clumsily within a day or two of hatching. Even so, they are not self-sufficient like the precocious chicks of the grouse and shorebird families and must be fed by their parents. The chicks recognize the unique sound of their parents' voices by the time they are four or five days old. Young ring-bills make their first flights when they are five weeks old, and the family breaks up sometime afterward.

〈 When trying to distinguish between different species of gulls it is important to note the markings on the bill, the eye color, and the color of the legs.

〈 *(opposite)* The record lifespan of a ring-bill is 31 years, although most live just 10 to 15 years.

FRANKLIN'S GULL *Larus pipixcan*

Family Details

Gull and Tern Family (Laridae), 97 species worldwide, 7 prairie species

See California Gull for a general discussion of the Gull and Tern Family.

Field Identification

A Franklin's gull is easy to identify since it is the only gull in the prairies with a black head. Early in the breeding season, the bird's breast and belly feathers are suffused with a delicate pink hue. Because of this subtle coloration, the naturalist on the Franklin Expedition of 1823 named it Franklin's rosy gull.

A Franklin's gull takes two years to reach full adult plumage. Even so, juveniles at the end of their first summer still look a lot like their parents.

Where to Find

The Franklin's gull nests on large marshes and sloughs throughout the northern Great Plains. At the end of the breeding season in the last half of July, the birds desert their nesting grounds and wander widely over the prairies for the rest of the summer, foraging in flooded fields, croplands, and native grasslands.

Wintering Grounds

The gulls leave the northern prairies in September and migrate to the western coast of Peru and northern Chile. The 14,000-kilometer (8,700-mi.) round-trip migration is one of the longest journeys made by any gull. En route, the gulls may gather in huge flocks. One November, an estimated 750,000 birds were recorded on Lake Texona, Texas, and one October, a phenomenal two and a half million Franklin's gulls darkened the skies above Salt Plains National Wildlife Refuge in Oklahoma.

Diet and Feeding Habits

Near its nesting colony, the Franklin's gull swoops for midges that swarm above the slough and also picks insects and aquatic invertebrates off the surface of the water. In the prairies, flocks of hungry Franklin's gulls follow the plow, diving through the dust to feed on grasshoppers, beetles, caterpillars, fly larvae, and earthworms.

Breeding Biology

These gulls nest in colonies with as few as 25 pairs but usually many more. Some very large colonies may include 100,000 nests, scattered among the cattails of a marsh. The location of these nests is hardly a secret as hundreds or thousands of birds scream and circle above the marsh. Their floating nest mound is made of cattails and bulrushes, the same kind favored by the American coot. Squabbling between the two species can be quite intense, and the irascible coot usually wins. The nesting gulls relentlessly compete with each other as well. If a pair is careless enough to leave their nest unguarded for an hour or more, the nest will likely be completely dismantled and stolen by the neighbors.

The gulls usually lay three olive-green eggs speckled and scrawled with brown, black, and gray. Like all gulls, both parents incubate and feed the young, which stay on the nest mound until they are around three weeks old. The young gulls begin to fly when they are five weeks old, and the family breaks up a week or two later.

< (top) It is surprising how large a cattail leaf a Franklin's gull will carry to its nest. (bottom) Climate scientists predict warming temperatures will cause many small prairie sloughs to permanently dry up, and upwards of 90 percent of prairie nesting Franklin's gulls may disappear within the next 20 years.

Both coots and black-crowned night-herons > will prey on unguarded gull eggs, and adult gulls must be wary of northern harriers during the day and great horned owls at night.

FORSTER'S TERN *Sterna forsteri*

Family Details

Gull and Tern Family (Laridae), 97 species worldwide, 7 prairie species

See California Gull for a general discussion of the Gull and Tern Family.

Field Identification

The Forster's tern has a deeply forked tail, black cap, orange legs, and an orange bill tipped with black. It is similar in size and color to the common tern, and even experienced birdwatchers mistake the two. Besides a slightly thicker bill, Forster's tern tends to nest in widely scattered colonies in cattails and bulrushes, whereas the common tern frequently nests in dense colonies on islands.

Where to Find

This handsome tern is uncommon and is found in localized sloughs and marshes throughout the prairies.

Wintering Grounds

Forster's terns leave the prairies in August. Most winter in the coastal regions of southern California and Mexico. They return again by mid-May.

Diet and Feeding Habits

It is a delight to watch these accomplished aeronauts hover gracefully, dive, and swoop over the still waters of a prairie slough. In a dive, the bird may disappear underwater completely only to surface almost immediately, clutching a silvery fish, a dragonfly nymph, or a water beetle in its colorful beak. In mid-flight, before they eat their catch, they usually shake themselves vigorously, producing a shower of water droplets that sparkles in the sun. The tern is equally adept at swooping over the water to pluck mayflies, water striders, and dead insects from the surface, without even wetting a wingtip.

Breeding Biology

During courtship, the male Forster's tern feeds his mate. Such courtship feeding is common among terns. The behavior strengthens the bond between the pair and also improves the female's nutritional condition and prepares her for the energetic demands of egg laying. Female terns that are fed less often by their mates produce lighter and fewer eggs. For a long time it was a mystery why underfed females did not simply feed themselves so that they could lay a full clutch of eggs. The probable reason is that a breeding female tern is too heavy to forage efficiently. An egg-heavy female weighs 50 percent more than she does at other times, and the added weight makes low-speed flight, hovering, and diving more difficult, so she relies on her mate to feed her.

Typically, Forster's terns nest in loose colonies in cattail sloughs and marshes. Usually, they build a floating mat of vegetation, but sometimes they use an old muskrat house or steal a nest from a grebe. The usual clutch of three eggs is incubated by both partners for roughly three weeks. While one bird sits on the nest, the other scans the skies overhead and defends their territory against trespassers. They aggressively dive-bomb Franklin's gulls and other terns. The chicks leave the nest a few days after hatching, as soon as they are able to swim, hide, and sneak through the cattails but are fed by their parents until they begin to fly.

Before a dive, a Forster's tern will ❯
often hover in place to locate a target.
Hovering is more common on windy
days when less energy is needed for
this strenuous hunting method.

BLACK TERN *Chlidonas niger*

Family Details

Gull and Tern Family (Laridae), 97 species worldwide, 7 prairie species

See California Gull for a general discussion of the Gull and Tern Family.

Field Identification

The distinctive black and gray plumage of this tern readily distinguishes it from other prairie terns, which all have white undersides. The legendary American ornithologist Arthur Cleveland Bent described the tern as "a restless waif of the air, flitting about hither and thither with a wayward, desultory flight, light and buoyant as a butterfly."

Where to Find

The black tern is found in wetlands throughout central North America but is most abundant in the fertile sloughs and marshes of the northern prairies.

Wintering Grounds

Adult terns may migrate south as early as the end of July, and juveniles follow a month later. Most winter along the Pacific Coast of Mexico and Central America and the northern coast of South America. In winter, the terns feed offshore, usually within 30 kilometers (18.5 mi.) of the coast. Flocks of a thousand birds or more may gather in good feeding areas. These delightful "marsh swallows" return to the prairies by the middle of May.

Diet and Feeding Habits

The black tern forages low over the water, usually within 3 meters (10 ft.) of the surface. This acrobatic flier skims spiders, beetles, and amphipods from the surface and snatches mayflies and moths from the swaying heads of cattails and bulrushes. It will even chase and outmaneuver fast-flying dragonflies. Black terns, unlike many other terns, rarely plunge-dive, preferring to hawk for their food on the wing.

Breeding Biology

Black terns mate with a new partner every season. Bachelor males begin to advertise for a mate with "food flights." The hopefuls fly low over the slough carrying a shiny beetle or large dragonfly and call out loudly to make themselves more conspicuous. Interested females follow and beg for the food. Once a pair has formed, the male continues to feed his new mate and copulation is almost always preceded by a gift of food. In one study, a male black tern, at the height of mating, fed his partner 14 times in two hours and mated with her three times.

The black tern nests in small, loose colonies in shallow marshes and sloughs and along the reed-covered margins of lakes. Colonies may contain up to 50 pairs, usually spaced between 5 to 20 meters (16 to 64 ft.) apart. The nests are small, flimsy piles of vegetation built in shallow water, and the eggs often become soaked. To combat this, black tern eggs have 50 percent more pores in their shells, an adaptation that keeps the inside of the eggs from becoming critically waterlogged.

Both sexes incubate the average clutch of three eggs, and they change places frequently, taking short shifts of just 30 to 60 minutes. When the chicks finally hatch after three weeks both adults brood and feed the young. The hard-working parents may deliver 46 damselflies to the nest in a single hour. The youngsters grow swiftly and make their first flight at around three weeks of age. By this time, the fledgling terns can feed themselves, but the parents may continue to supplement the young birds' diets for several weeks afterward.

❮ The black tern is an agile flier that will skim the water surface in the manner of a swallow, doggedly pursue a dragonfly on a zigzag chase, and vigorously engage a rival in a energetic dogfight.

For several weeks, adult doves feed their ›
newly hatched young a protein- and
fat-rich milk-like substance secreted
from the wall of their crop that has the
consistency of cottage cheese.

MOURNING DOVE *Zenaida macroura*

Family Details

Pigeon and Dove Family (Columbidae), 308 species worldwide,
2 prairie species

Everyone who has seen a pigeon in a city park can recall the
general appearance of the birds in this large family. Pigeons and
doves vary greatly in size, but all have a small head, a compact
body, short legs, and a short beak. Some doves are no larger
than a sparrow, while some pigeons, such as the crowned
pigeon of New Guinea, are as large as a turkey.

Most pigeons and doves are strong fliers, and many have
very large flight muscles, comprising up to 44 percent of their
body weight, one of the highest proportions in any group of
birds. Compare this with grebes, which are at the other extreme.
Heavy-bodied grebes are weak fliers with skimpy flight muscles
that make up just 14 percent of their body weight.

One of the most intriguing aspects of the biology of pigeons
and doves is their habit of feeding their young with "milk." This
highly nutritious food, which resembles cottage cheese, has
more than twice as much fat and seven times as much protein
as cow's milk. Both parents produce the specialized milk in their
crops and regurgitate the rich food to their newly hatched chicks.

Field Identification

The mourning dove is a streamlined, robin-sized bird that is grayish
brown above and tan underneath. The dove takes flight with
a characteristic whistling flutter, and, when flying, the white
edges of its long, tapered tail are clearly visible. At close range,
you may notice the bluish skin around the bird's eyes and its dull
red feet and legs. The dove produces a soft, mournful croon that
is the origin of its common name.

Where to Find

The mourning dove is widespread throughout the prairies. It is
equally at home in native grasslands, farmlands, and urban parks
but avoids thick stands of trees.

Wintering Grounds

The doves of the northern Great Plains generally winter throughout
the central and southern United States. In recent years, the popularity
of bird feeders has encouraged some of these hardy birds to winter
on the prairies. Mourning doves can withstand extreme cold temperatures if they have an ample supply of food, but their toes can
become frostbitten, and sometimes their fleshy feet freeze to the
metal on bird feeders; such doves must be rescued.

Diet and Feeding Habits

The mourning dove's diet consists almost exclusively of the
seeds of grasses, wildflowers, and farm crops. Typically, it feeds
on the ground, quickly filling its crop, then flies to a roost away
from predators to slowly digest its meal. Seeds are swallowed
whole and are ground up in its muscular gizzard with the aid of
grit and gravel, which the birds ingest for this purpose.

Breeding Biology

Flocks of mourning doves return to the prairies in late April or
early May. Each hopeful male may coo from a dozen different
perches trying to lure a mate to his side. When an interested
female lands near him, he coos even louder, dips and bows,
and gently nibbles the feathers on her head and neck, trying to
convince her that he is the dandiest dove of them all.

The mourning dove builds a flimsy nest of grass stems and
twigs. In the prairies, I have found nests on the ground, but
more often they are in thick shrubbery. The caragana bushes and
conifers planted as shelterbelts around farmhouses are a common
nest site. Normally, the doves lay two bright white eggs, which the
adults must cover continuously because they are so conspicuous.
The male and female share the two-week incubation, and both
parents feed the nestlings "crop milk" until the young are three or
four days old. The young doves, called squabs, fledge after another
two weeks by which time they are fed nothing but seeds. The
male parent continues to feed the squabs for another 12 days after
they fledge, while the female prepares to lay a second clutch of
eggs. In the southern United States, a female mourning dove may
lay five or six clutches in a single nesting season; in the northern
prairies, two is probably the maximum.

‹ A long-eared owl never builds a nest and instead uses the old nest of a hawk or crow. In this case, the owl has settled on the collapsed nest of a black-billed magpie.

LONG-EARED OWL *Asio otus*

Family Details

Owl Family (Strigidae), 180 species worldwide, 10 prairie species

Owls, with their big eyes and large, swiveling heads, are recognizable to everyone. They are mainly nocturnal birds of prey and have evolved an array of adaptations to hunt in darkness. The retina of an owl's eye, for example, is densely packed with sensitive light detectors that enable the bird to see well at night, although, as a trade-off, it probably has somewhat weaker color vision. The feathers on its face are shaped like a disk that concentrates sounds and increases the sensitivity of the bird's hearing. As well, in some species, the external ear openings are at slightly different heights on the sides of the bird's head. This helps the owl to more accurately pinpoint sounds and capture prey in complete darkness.

Owls, like most birds of prey, have a sharp, hooked beak and strong, talon-tipped feet. The birds generally swallow their prey whole and regurgitate the indigestible parts of a meal as compact pellets several hours later.

The sexes look very similar in most species of owls. Nearly all have plumage that is a cryptic mix of brown, gray, black, tan, and white. The body feathers of the birds are surprisingly soft, and the edges of their wing feathers have a comb-like fringe.

Both of these features help to muffle sound and make their flight as quiet as a heartbeat.

Field Identification

The long-eared owl may be confused with the larger great horned owl since both birds have a rusty colored facial disk, bright yellow eyes, and long feathered ear tufts. The long-eared owl is a smaller, more secretive owl. Its ear tufts are closer together and more upright than those of the great horned owl whose ear tufts point outward and are spaced farther apart.

Where to Find

The long-eared owl is found throughout the prairies in wooded coulees and river valleys. This elusive raptor is strictly nocturnal and is seldom seen, although I once found a long-eared owl perched on a fence post in broad daylight. This was an extremely unusual owl, and I have never found another one like it. Most often these owls spend the day hidden in thick vegetation, especially conifers, where they perch close to the trunk and rely on the vertical streaking in their plumage to camouflage them.

Wintering Grounds

Although some long-eared owls may winter in the prairies, many of them, especially the more northern birds, migrate to the gentler climes farther south in the central and southern United States. Some migrate even farther. An owl banded in Saskatchewan was later recovered in Oaxaca, Mexico, 4,000 kilometers (2,485 mi.) away.

Diet and Feeding Habits

The long-eared owl likes to nest and roost in dense vegetation, although it forages in open habitats, such as fields and meadows. It has large wings for its size and hunts by systematically coursing back and forth close to the ground, sometimes hovering when it needs extra time to pinpoint a small rodent hidden in the grass. The owl has particularly sensitive hearing and relies as much, if not more, on hearing than it does on vision to locate and capture prey in darkness.

The long-eared owl is primarily a small mammal specialist, preying on ground squirrels, voles, deer mice, pocket mice, kangaroo rats, pocket gophers, and at least four kinds of bats. Occasionally, the owl also hunts songbirds, lizards, and small snakes.

‹ Scientists believe the facial disk in owls helps to collect sound waves in the manner of a parabolic antenna and focuses them at the ear opening.

Breeding Biology

The breeding season for long-eared owls begins in March and April. The female owl does all the incubation, and she is likely the one that selects the nest site. In an Idaho study, most of the owls chose to set up house in the old stick nests of black-billed magpies and crows. The new tenants generally make no renovations to the nest, although a few feathers may get added to the lining. The female owl sheds feathers from an area on her belly, which becomes the bare brood patch used to heat her eggs. The feathers from her brood patch are those used to line the nest.

A long-eared owl may lay as many as eight glossy white eggs, but a clutch of four or five is more common. Throughout the month-long incubation, the male feeds his mate. The female remains on the eggs almost constantly, except for an occasional short break or two at night when darkness makes the eggs less vulnerable to detection by predators. The male continues to provision his entire family for two weeks after the chicks hatch, while the female broods the young. The young owlets can fly and hunt for themselves when they are two months old, and by this time both parents have deserted them.

❮ Young long-eared owls leave the nest
many weeks before they can fly and
shelter separately from their nest mates,
reducing their vulnerability to predators.

SHORT-EARED OWL *Asio flammeus*

Family Details

Owl Family (Strigidae), 180 species worldwide, 10 prairie species
See Long-eared Owl for a general discussion of the Owl Family.

Field Identification

The short-eared owl might better be called the no-eared owl since the small feathered tufts on its head are rarely visible. Watch for a pale streaked long broad winged owl that often hunts during the day. Its flight is moth-like and buoyant as it glides and flaps close to the ground. The owl flies very much like the northern harrier, but the two birds can be distinguished by the large white rump patch that is clearly visible on the harrier.

Where to Find

The short-eared is an open country owl that hunts and nests in grasslands, marshes, sloughs, and stubble fields. The bird is a gypsy and moves around searching for concentrations of voles. Owl numbers vary dramatically from year to year in direct relationship with the rise and fall of the local rodent population. During a vole plague, for example, several thousand owls may be present in an area, and the following year there may be none.

Wintering Grounds

Most short-eared owls from the Canadian prairies migrate into the United States. Sometimes they overwinter in loose groups of up to 200 birds. These winter owl gatherings usually result from a local abundance of prey.

Diet and Feeding Habits

The life and times of the prairie short-eared owl are closely tied to vole numbers, which follow a three- to four-year cycle similar to that of Arctic lemmings. When voles are abundant, the owls may hunt nothing else but these furry rodents. When voles are scarce, short-eareds will hunt moles, shrews, weasels, pocket gophers, and mice. They will also catch small numbers of songbirds and shorebirds. The short-eared owl, in common with most owls, is a visual and acoustic hunter using both eyesight and hearing to locate its prey.

The short-eared owl has noticeably large wings for its size. In the jargon of aeronautical engineering, the owl has very low wing-loading, and this benefits the bird in several ways. It gives the owl better aerial agility and also a slow flight speed, which allows it more time to scan the ground. The low wing-loading also lessens the noise of its wings so that it can hear better in flight and is less likely to frighten its prey.

The short-eared owl frequently hunts and nests in the same habitats as those used by the northern harrier, and the two raptors are often antagonistic to each other. There are many records of owls chasing harriers, and harriers harassing owls and pirating their prey. In the end, the owl rules at night and the harrier during the day.

Breeding Biology

The male short-eared owl frequently courts his mate during the day, so the details of his "sky dance" are well known. With the attentive female sitting on the ground, the displaying male quickly climbs in the sky through a series of small circles. Once he is about 60 to 90 meters up (200 to 300 ft.), he dives steeply, clapping his wings five to ten times beneath his body. Throughout the aerial performance, the male hoots continuously. At the bottom of the dive the male swoops skyward and starts to circle and climb all over again. Short-eared owls pair with a different partner every breeding season, and it is important for a male to perform well to attract a mate.

The short-eared owl nests on the ground, usually on dry prairie or in a stubble field. Typically, the nest is a hollow scrape sparsely lined with grasses and downy feathers. When food is plentiful, the owls may nest in loose colonies. In a Montana study, the researchers found 30 nests in an area of just 164 hectares (405 ac.). Two of the nests were just 55 meters (180 ft.) apart.

A well-fed short-eared owl may lay as many as 14 glossy white eggs. The hardworking male provisions his mate during the entire month-long incubation and then feeds the chicks as well until they are large enough to be left uncovered by the female. The young owlets leave the nest after two weeks but do not fly until they are roughly a month old. The parents continue to feed the youngsters for several weeks after fledging.

GREAT HORNED OWL *Bubo virginianus*

Family Details

Owl Family (Strigidae), 180 species worldwide, 10 prairie species
See Long-eared Owl for a general discussion of the Owl Family.

Field Identification

The great horned owl is one of the most inspiring birds of prey on the prairies. Whether sitting on a nest or flying, it looks huge. It has a body weight of 1.8 kilograms (4 lb.) and a 1.6-meter (63-in.) wingspan. Among owls, only the snowy is heavier and more powerful. The great horned owl's bright yellow eyes and long ear tufts distinguish it from all other large owls, and its size and bulk alone separate it from the smaller and slimmer long-eared owl.

Where to Find

The horned hooter is the most widespread owl in the Americas, ranging from the Arctic treeline in North America to the windy pampas of Argentina in South America. This large adaptable owl is a relatively common resident of the prairies, found in wooded coulees, badlands, farm shelterbelts, and urban woodlands. It is nocturnal and during the day hides motionless in a tree or thick shrubbery.

Wintering Grounds

The hardy great horned owl is a year-round citizen of the prairies. In *The Birds of Alberta*, authors Ray and Jim Salt wrote, "In winter, conifers are often chosen for daytime roosts since they provide shelter from the wind and snow, as well as from the eyes of magpies and jays that are always ready to mob a sleepy owl."

Diet and Feeding Habits

This large powerful owl is a threat to a great variety of furred and feathered creatures on the prairies. It hunts cottontails, jackrabbits, ground squirrels, pocket gophers, voles, mice, red fox pups, muskrats, and, sometimes, house cats. Even the noxious spray of the striped skunk does not deter this taloned terror of the coulees. Remarkably, the great horned owl will even attack and kill porcupines. Punishment was dealt to one owl that had 84 quills embedded in its face, sides, and legs.

The versatile great horned owl also hunts ducks, coots, pheasants, grouse, crows, blue jays, gulls, shorebirds, grebes, bitterns, and even great blue herons. In the Sonoran Desert of Baja California, Mexico, I once flushed a great horned owl just after it had killed an adult peregrine falcon. On the northern prairies, the rapacious owls also hunt these fast-flying falcons as well as other raptors, including prairie falcons, long-eared owls, short-eared owls, burrowing owls, and red-tailed hawks.

Breeding Biology

The great horned owl is the earliest bird to nest on the prairies, sometimes laying eggs in the last week of February, when winter still firmly grips the land. Like all owls, the great horned never builds its own nest, preferring to use a natural cavity in a cliff face or the old abandoned nest of a crow, raven, or hawk. Occasionally, it will even nest on the ground, and their aggressiveness insures that only the boldest, or most foolish, of predators would dare to approach such a nest. Several times I have been attacked by a great horned owl when I tried to photograph its nest in a tree, but I always wore a helmet and protective clothing and was never injured. In *The Owls of North America*, author Allan Eckert described others who were not so fortunate:

> There is no dearth of tales about the incredible savagery with which the great horned owl attacks a foe or defends itself, nor is there need for exaggeration of any kind. There are scores of well-authenticated cases on record where men have been blinded and suffered severe injuries to head, throat, chest, back, and groin by enraged attacking great horned owls. The attacks are bold, slashing, and very dangerous, made even more so by the total unexpectedness with which they strike.

The great horned owl usually lays a clutch of two or three white eggs, which the female incubates alone for roughly 30 days, while her smaller mate hunts and feeds her. Young owlets begin to fly when they are seven weeks old, but take another three weeks to become proficient. Learning to hunt takes even longer, and the young fledglings may be fed by their parents well into the summer.

SNOWY OWL *Bubo scandiaca*

Family Details

Owl Family (Strigidae), 180 species worldwide, 10 prairie species
See Long-eared Owl for a general discussion of the Owl Family.

Field Identification

The snowy owl is a large white owl with penetrating golden yellow
eyes. An adult female may weigh nearly 3 kilograms (6.6 lb.) and
have a wingspan of 1.8 meters (5.9 ft.), making it the heaviest,
most powerful owl in North America. The plumage of most adult
males is almost pure white, whereas that of many adult females is
barred and spotted with dark brown.

Where to Find

The snowy is a welcome winter visitor to the prairies. Telephone
poles are a popular hunting perch for these owls, and an afternoon
drive along a prairie highway in winter may yield half a dozen
sightings or more.

Wintering Grounds

When food is available, many snowy owls, especially territorial
males, remain in their Arctic breeding grounds for the winter
enduring blizzards, numbing cold, and weeks of continuous
darkness. When the lemming population crashes, great numbers
of these magnificent owls migrate into the northern Great Plains.
In exceptional years, a few snowy owls may even fly as far south
as Florida, Texas, and central California.

Diet and Feeding Habits

The "tundra ghost" of the Arctic has always fascinated me,
and I have watched these birds numerous times on their Arctic
breeding grounds. I wrote about them in *A is for Arctic: Natural
Wonders of a Polar World:*

The snowy owl preys on lemmings, and indeed, the bird may eat
three to five of the small furry rodents a day, consuming 600 to 1,600
of them in a single year. In a four-month summer nesting season, a
pair of adult snowy owls and their brood of six to eight chicks may
gulp down as many as 2,600 lemmings and still be hungry for more.
Somehow, though, this heavyweight owl with its large, powerful
feet and strong, sharpened talons, seems a little over armed to tackle
the lightweight lemming, which is a skimpy 70 grams (2.5 oz.).

The reason for the heavy-duty weaponry becomes clear when
the owl migrates to the prairies in winter. There they may hunt
jackrabbits and cottontails, grouse, pheasants, ducks, and geese.
One winter, on the outskirts of Vancouver, the big owls specialized
in house cats.

The most common hunting tactic used by the snowy owl is
simply to sit and wait. With this method, the bird monitors a stretch
of terrain from an elevated vantage point, then launches an attack
once a vulnerable victim is spotted.

Breeding Biology

Snowy owls breed from the Arctic treeline north to the limit of land.
One August, I photographed a pair of downy owl chicks on northern

Ellesmere Island, just 150 kilometers (93 mi.) from the northern tip of the continent. Male snowy owls set up breeding territories in April, and the females begin to lay eggs in late May. The number of eggs she lays depends on the lemming population. In years when the rodents are scarce, the female may lay no eggs at all, but in boom years she may have a clutch of 11. The young owlets leave the nest when they are 25 days old and continue to be fed entirely by their parents for at least another five weeks, when they finally begin to hunt for themselves. Even then, the inexperienced young owls are partially fed for several more weeks.

→ Trivia Tidbit

All owls regurgitate compact pellets of indigestible hair, feathers, bones, teeth, claws, and insect parts, three to 12 hours after they have eaten. A large owl, such as the great-horned owl, may spit up a pellet 13 centimeters (5 in.) long and shaped like a stubby cigar, whereas the pellets from a burrowing owl are usually pencil-thin and just 3 centimeters (1.2 in.) long. An owl will often regurgitate pellets where it regularly roosts, and these may accumulate on the ground. In prairie Alberta, Aubrey collected more than 50 great-horned owl pellets beneath a single roost tree. The dissection of pellets is the principle way biologists study an owl's diet.

Owl pellet analysis is also one of the best ways for researchers to survey small mammals. Because owls hunt such a broad range of prey, they are better at sampling the different rodents that live in an area than a biologist is with live traps.

BURROWING OWL *Athene cunicularia*

Family Details

Owl Family (Strigidae), 180 species worldwide, 10 prairie species
See Long-eared Owl for a general discussion of the Owl Family.

Field Identification

The burrowing owl is a small owl, only 23 centimeters (9 in.) tall, with long legs, yellow eyes, and no ear tufts. The bird usually roosts on the ground but sometimes perches on fence posts.

Where to Find

This owl is an uncommon resident of short-grass and mixed-grass prairies throughout the Great Plains. The Committee on the Status of Endangered Wildlife in Canada (COSEWIC) lists it as endangered in Canada. A 2017 report states: owl surveys suggest a continuing significant decrease in density in all areas of prairie Canada over the last 40 years, including a 90% population decline from 1990 to 2000, and further declines from 2005–2015 of 76% in Saskatchewan and 45% in Alberta … Based on rates of decline since 2004, population estimates as of 2015 were 106 in Saskatchewan and 148 in Alberta.

Farther south in the United States, burrowing owl populations are stable in Colorado, New Mexico, and Texas—the core of the species' range.

A multitude of factors are responsible for the drastic declines: conversion of grassland to cropland, fragmentation of remaining grasslands, prey declines resulting from the use of rodenticides and insecticides, climate change, and collisions with vehicles.

Wintering Grounds

Burrowing owls leave the northern Great Plains between early September and mid-October. Birds from the Canadian prairies, Montana, and North Dakota migrate as least as far south as Texas and northern Mexico. From the recovery of bands, it seems that Canadian burrowing owls may migrate farther south than owls in the United States, suggesting a "leap frog" migration. These charming little owls return to the northern prairies in April.

Diet and Feeding Habits

The burrowing owl, like the short-eared owl, is another prairie owl that hunts in the daytime as well as at night. During the day, these insect exterminators prey on dung beetles, carrion beetles, crickets, and grasshoppers in the vicinity of their nest. One spring,

I spent nine hours watching a mother owl resting on the mound at the mouth of her nest burrow. Throughout that day, the vigilant mother repeatedly sprinted across the prairie on pencil-thin legs to slam a taloned foot on a large juicy grasshopper that had made the fatal mistake of landing nearby.

At night, their diet switches to rodents, with deer mice and voles as the most common prey. During their nocturnal hunts, the owls forage farther away from the nest, up to 5 kilometers (3 mi.) away.

Breeding Biology

The burrowing owl, as its name suggests, nests underground. The male and female work together to renovate the abandoned burrow of a ground squirrel, prairie dog, or badger. The pair dig with their beaks and kick the dirt backward with their feet.

Commonly, the nest burrow consists of a tunnel, 2 to 3 meters (6.5 to 10 ft.) in length, with an enlarged chamber at the end. In Alberta, and other areas, the owls have the unusual habit of lining the tunnel and nest chamber with dried, shredded cattle manure. A researcher in Oregon speculates that the manure masks the owls' odor and hides their presence from keen-nosed predators, such as badgers and foxes. The manure may also attract dung

beetles and provide the owls, especially youngsters, with a handy source of food.

A pair of burrowing owls may raise three to eleven chicks. When chicks inside the burrow are frightened they will mimic the buzzing sound of an angry rattlesnake. This interesting alarm vocalization may deter mammalian predators. The young owlets first emerge from the burrow when they are two weeks old, and in Alberta this happens from the middle of June onward.

As the youngsters grow, they cluster around the mouth of the burrow waiting for the adults to feed them. While they are waiting, they hop about and flap their fluffy wings, preen each other, pick at debris on the ground, and chase beetles that crawl nearby. Young burrowing owls can fly by the time they are six weeks old.

Because burrowing owls are so small and nest on the ground, they are preyed upon by many predators. In Alberta, the list includes badgers, coyotes, red foxes, striped skunks, least and long-tailed weasels, prairie rattlesnakes, and bullsnakes. Other predators attack from the sky, including Swainson's hawks, ferruginous hawks, northern harriers, prairie falcons, great horned owls, and short-eared owls. The burrowing owl is clearly the most hunted avian predator on the prairies.

‹ This adult burrowing owl was delivering a burying beetle (*Nicrophorus* sp.), a common prey item, to its large family of seven chicks that were huddled around the family burrow in southern Alberta.

COMMON NIGHTHAWK *Chordeiles minor*

Family Details

Nightjar Family (Caprimulgidae), 89 species worldwide, 2 prairie species

The unusual common name for members of this family is derived from their tendency to be active mainly after dark and to produce loud calls that "jar" the silence of the night. Another common name for the family is goatsuckers, an equally intriguing moniker. This name comes from an ancient superstition dating from the time of Aristotle. All of the nightjars have a tiny beak but a very wide gape, and peasant farmers believed the birds clamped their large mouth to the udders of their livestock and milked them dry. In fact, nightjars are strict insect eaters, and they net their prey on the wing using their large mouth. Since these birds sometimes swoop near grazing livestock to catch flying insects flushed by the animals, they were blamed for the poor milk production of the undernourished, pest-ridden farm animals. The stomach of an average nightjar is the size of a thimble, and it would take quite a flock of these birds to milk a goat dry, not to mention the trouble they would have convincing an irascible old nanny to stand still while all this was happening.

Field Identification

The nighthawk is most often seen in flight. The grayish brown, robin-sized bird has long pointed wings, each with a wide band of white in the center of the underwing. No other bird on the prairies has these conspicuous white wing bars. If you are lucky

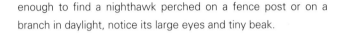

‹ The cryptic plumage of the nighthawk allows the bird to be well camouflaged when it roosts on the mottled ground of the prairies.

The poorwill, as in all goatsuckers, › has short, weak legs and feet.

enough to find a nighthawk perched on a fence post or on a branch in daylight, notice its large eyes and tiny beak.

Where to Find

A nighthawk might be found in any habitat in the prairies and even in the center of a city. Formerly, these birds were common in urban centers because they would nest on flat gravel roofs and hawk for insects between the towering buildings. In recent years, these harmless birds have disappeared from many cities. Since the late 1960s, nighthawks have slowly declined, and their population size now numbers less than half of what it was. In the Prairie Provinces, pesticide spraying for mosquitoes and the loss and alteration of native prairies to cultivation, fire suppression, and cattle grazing are believed to be the primary factors responsible for the decline.

Wintering Grounds

Prairie nighthawks winter in distant South America, mainly in Paraguay, Uruguay, and northern Argentina—a round trip of 16,000 kilometers (9,940 mi.).

Diet and Feeding Habits

The common nighthawk has a simple diet containing all the major food groups: insects, insects, and more insects. Flying ants are the most common food, but the bird also scoops up beetles, bugs, and flies. One investigator examined a nighthawk that had eaten 2,175 flying ants. Another bird had 500 mosquitoes in its stomach.

At one time, scientists believed that the nighthawk used echo-location to pinpoint insects in flight, but it now appears that it relies entirely on its sensitive vision. The eyes of all birds are relatively large, but those of the nighthawk are exceptionally so. In fact, the nighthawk's eyes weigh more than its brain.

Breeding Biology

The common nighthawk is silent most of the year except during the breeding season in June and early July when males court and "boom." Typically, an interested female sits on the ground like a spectator at an air show while her suitor performs in the sky above her. A nighthawk's boom sounds like someone blowing across the top of an empty bottle, and the sound is produced at the bottom of a power dive as air rushes through the stiff feathers at the tip of the male's wings. An enthusiastic boomer may dive 40 times in half an hour.

The nighthawk lays its two patterned eggs directly on the bare ground. The female incubates the eggs alone and leaves them unattended at night to feed. During the day, she covers the eggs continuously to protect them from the excessive heat of the sun. In the badlands of Alberta, for example, the ground temperature may exceed 50°C (122°F), and would quickly cook an exposed nighthawk egg. An incubating female cools herself, and her eggs, by evaporating moisture from the lining of her cavernous mouth, which is richly supplied with blood vessels for this purpose.

Nighthawk chicks are cryptically covered with down and can scuttle about soon after hatching. The male does most of the feeding of the twins, while the female broods them. The precocious young can fly before they are three weeks old.

→ **Trivia Tidbit**

The common poorwill (*Phalaenoptilus nuttallii*) is closely related to the nighthawk and in Canada is restricted to shrubby grasslands in the Cypress Hills in southwest Saskatchewan and southeast Alberta. The poorwill is the only bird known to hibernate. When the migratory poorwill is in Canada between April and September, it can periodically slip into a deep torpor where its body temperature drops from a normal 40°C (104°F) to a mere 5°C (41°F) and may remain "chilled out" for up to 36 hours. Doing so saves the bird valuable energy when temperatures are cool or insect prey is scarce. It's on the birds' wintering grounds in the southwest United States that their use of torpor is most profound. There, they may slip into a long-term torpor lasting weeks and sometimes months at a stretch, enjoying the same energy savings as does a hibernating chipmunk or woodchuck. The poorwill's unusual behavior prompted the Hopi Indians of Arizona to call it "the sleeping one."

BELTED KINGFISHER *Ceryle alcyon*

Family Details

Kingfisher Family (Alcedinidae) 91 species worldwide, 1 prairie species

This is a family of small to medium-sized birds that hover and dive for fish; snatch insects on the wing; and scoop lizards, snakes, and scorpions off the ground. They have stocky bodies, short necks, large heads, and long, thick pointed bills. Many are brightly colored in cinnamon and vibrant azure blue.

All of these handsome birds nest in holes of one kind or another, either in a riverbank, a tree, or a termite mound, and most of them lay glossy white eggs. In the darkened interior of a nest cavity, white eggs can be found more easily by the parents, and there is no need to camouflage them from predators since they are hidden inside a cavity.

Most kingfishers are noisy and produce loud, shrill shrieks or chattering rattles. The boisterous call of Australia's laughing kookaburra is famous and has been used in countless Hollywood movies to depict the tropics. The kookaburra is one of the world's largest kingfishers.

The rusty band across the belly of the lower ❯ bird identifies it as a female kingfisher.
Photo © Shutterstock Steven Blandin *(top)*
Shutterstock Collins93 *(bottom)*

Field Identification

The belted kingfisher is a medium-sized bird with a large ragged crest. The bird is bluish gray on top and white underneath and has a broad white collar. Both sexes have a bluish gray band across their chests, and the female has a rusty band across her belly as well. Generally, the kingfisher flies off in alarm and rattles loudly at the slightest disturbance, so you will probably hear the bird before you see it.

Where to Find

The noisy kingfisher may be found on any stream, river, pond, or lake in the prairies. The bird avoids muddy waters and those that are overgrown with vegetation, both of which make diving for fish more difficult.

Wintering Grounds

If there is open water for fishing, the bird can survive the cold of a prairie winter. Even so, most kingfishers migrate south in October to the coastal and inland waters of Mexico and Central America. The bird's familiar scolding rattle returns to the prairies in April.

Diet and Feeding Habits

Although the kingfisher is primarily a piscivore, or fish-eater, it also catches frogs, snakes, lizards, snails, and crayfish. Typically, the big-beaked bird hunts from a perch, usually a tree snag, a branch, or a telephone wire overhanging the water. It may also course along the shore, hover, and scan. Most of its fishing is done near the surface, and usually the kingfisher does not completely submerge in a dive. At the moment of impact, the bird closes its eyes and grabs the fish with its pincer-like beak. It carries the wiggling prey to a branch where it repeatedly pounds it against the wood. This compulsory "tenderizing" breaks the spines off catfish and sticklebacks and stuns the prey so that it can be swallowed headfirst in a single gulp. Kingfishers, in common with birds of prey, disgorge compact pellets of undigested bones and fish scales after they have eaten. Biologists dissect these pellets to learn which fish the birds are eating.

Breeding Biology

The kingfisher nests in a hole, usually in a bank along a shoreline, but occasionally in a gravel pit or a roadcut, far from water. Both adults peck and shovel for up to a week to dig a tunnel one to two meters (3 to 6 ft.) deep, with a small round chamber at the end. On shorelines, the tunnel entrance is dug high enough above the water to avoid flooding, yet far enough below the top of the bank to keep predators from sneaking inside.

The birds lay five to seven glossy white eggs, which both parents incubate for the 22 days it takes for the pink, naked nestlings to hatch. Researcher Michael Hamas jokingly remarked that the homely youngsters "chatter continuously and huddle together, forming a cluster of interlocking heads and wings."

Young kingfisher chicks do not produce feces packaged in a convenient mucous sack that can be carried away by the parents as is common in most songbirds. Instead, they point their butts at the wall and squirt away. Afterward, they spin around and peck the earth above where they blasted. This loosens the soil, which buries the feces and keeps the nest chamber relatively clean. The fledglings leave the nest burrow at a month of age and are fed by both parents for three weeks afterward.

⟨ The red nape on the top photograph identifies it as a male downy woodpecker.

DOWNY AND HAIRY WOODPECKERS

Picoides pubescens and Picoides villosus

Family Details

Woodpecker Family (Picidae) 210 species worldwide, 5 prairie species

Woodpeckers are the original head-bangers. Their unique arboreal lifestyle has produced a number of special adaptations. They have a reinforced skull to protect their brain when they are drilling for food, and a strong, chisel-like bill. Many of them have a long tongue that extends far beyond the tip of their bill. The tongue is coated with sticky saliva and tipped with barbs to extract wood-boring grubs from crevices and ants from nests. The birds also have stiff, pointed tail feathers to prop themselves up and strong legs muscles to stay anchored when they start to hammer.

Most of these hard-headed carpenters nest in holes that they excavate in the trunks of trees. Afterward, their abandoned holes are used for shelter and as nest sites by a wide variety of birds, mammals, frogs, and snakes. Because old woodpecker holes are crucial to so many other animals the birds are often designated as a "keystone" species.

Woodpeckers are the only birds to drum rhythmically with their beaks to proclaim their territories and advertise for mates. Normally, both sexes hammer on hollow, resonant branches and snags. Some of these hammerheads have discovered the marvel of metal, and they drum on eavestroughs, drainpipes, and trash cans, testing the patience of the most understanding homeowner.

Field Identification

The downy and hairy woodpeckers have very similar feather markings and can be a challenge to differentiate. Both have two white stripes on the side of their head, one above the eye and the other below. They have an all-white chest and belly, a black back with a vertical white stripe, and black wings with white spots. The males in both woodpeckers have a patch of red on the nape of their neck. The downy is considerably smaller than the hairy, but size is difficult to evaluate unless the two birds are seen together. The length of each bird's beak is a good way to distinguish between them. The downy's beak is distinctly shorter than its head, whereas the hairy's beak is the same size.

Where to Find

Both woodpeckers are equally at home in urban forests or wooded coulees and are frequent visitors to backyard bird feeders.

Wintering Grounds

Both woodpeckers are year-round residents of the prairies and are a welcome sight on a winter stroll.

Diet and Feeding Habits

Both the hairy and the downy forage on tree trunks and large limbs where they search for adult wood-boring beetles and their larvae, caterpillars, ants, spiders, and millipedes. They poke and peer into crevices and remove bits of bark to reach hidden prey. They will rapidly tap along a branch or trunk, searching for differences in the resonance that might betray a hidden insect tunnel. Once a tunnel is located they chisel away the overlying wood to capture the prey. Roughly a quarter of the diet of each woodpecker is plant material, especially berries and seeds. Both will also steal the sugary fluid from the holes that sapsuckers purposefully drill for sap.

Breeding Biology

One of the unique characteristics of all woodpeckers is their use of drumming to communicate. Everyone has heard the characteristic hollow hammering on a tree snag or branch, and if you are like me, you assumed it was a pumped-up male advertising his virility to rival males and prospective female mates. It turns out that woodpeckers hammer their hearts out for many reasons other than this, and females may drum as often as males. In winter, a pair of woodpeckers will usually roost overnight in separate tree cavities to shelter from the weather. At dawn, mates may drum to each other to coordinate a rendezvous. Both sexes may also drum when an intruder enters their territory, and, in this instance, it seems the drumming is a displacement behavior meant to work off anxiety. When woodpeckers are feeling relaxed and content, they may drum between preening bouts. Either sex may also drum to notify their partner that they wish to mate. It's a little like Tarzan beating

his chest. One January, in Saskatchewan, I saw a pair of hairy woodpeckers drumming for yet another reason. The drumming of one woodpecker stimulated a burst from its partner. The duet lasted nearly 10 minutes, and the two birds each drummed at least half a dozen times. Hairy woodpeckers pair in midwinter, and the drumming duet was probably a means to reinforce the pair bond during the three to four months before the nesting season began.

For a human, the drum roll of one woodpecker is hard to distinguish from that of another. A California researcher recorded the drums of 11 different species of woodpeckers and then analyzed them. He discovered that the drumming sequences were unique for each species. The main difference was in the number of beats per second and also whether the drum sequence sped up, slowed down, or remained steady. Downy woodpeckers tap at 17 beats per second, and slow down, whereas hairy woodpeckers drum at a steady 26 beats per second. Of course, the human ear cannot detect these subtle differences, but luckily the woodpeckers can. Such subtle communication methods demonstrate that woodpeckers aren't boneheads after all.

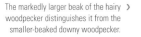
The markedly larger beak of the hairy ❯ woodpecker distinguishes it from the smaller-beaked downy woodpecker.

— 175 —

NORTHERN FLICKER *Colaptes auratus*

Family Details

Woodpecker Family (Picidae) 210 species worldwide, 5 prairie species

Field Identification

The flicker is a medium-sized brown woodpecker with black barring on its back, a black bib, and black spots on its belly. The flicker has two color variations. In the "yellow-shafted" variety the underwings are bright yellow, both sexes have a patch of red on the nape of their neck, and the male has a black moustache. In the "red-shafted" variety the underwings are reddish in color, the male has a red moustache, but neither sex has a red patch on its neck.

Where to Find

The northern flicker is a common, noisy resident of open woodlands and suburban areas throughout the prairies. The yellow-shafted variety exists in the central and eastern prairies and is replaced in the extreme west by the red-shafted variety. There is a broad zone of overlap between the two species where hybridization occurs, making identification challenging.

Wintering Grounds

Flickers from the northern prairies migrate to the southern United States in October, returning to their breeding grounds in late March and early April.

Diet and Feeding Habits

In summer, the flicker may forage on tree trunks in the usual woodpecker fashion, but most of the time, it hunts on the ground, hopping about, hammering and probing anthills with its powerful beak. The northern flicker eats more ants than any other bird in North America. Of interest to those readers who love avian trivia, as I do, the name for a creature whose principal diet is ants and termites is a myrmecophage. Now that's a challenging word to casually slip into any conversation.

Although they are ant specialists, flickers also eat ground beetles, crickets, wood lice, grasshoppers, butterflies, grubs, bugs, and caterpillars. In autumn, when most ants have moved underground, the birds' diet shifts to wild fruits including those of sumac, dogwood, and poison ivy.

❮ This male red-shafted flicker was alarmed and agitated by a bullsnake climbing its nest tree. The snake eventually found the opening to the nest cavity and disappeared inside where chicks were calling.

Breeding Biology

Researcher Lawrence Kilham compared the sound of a flicker drumming to a miniature pneumatic drill. During the breeding season, the paired birds each drum at established posts throughout their territory. The drum rolls, which contain roughly 25 beats, last a second, although you would need a sonograph to recognize this. Even so, the birds can tell the difference and, as mentioned earlier, each species of woodpecker has a unique drumming pattern.

Flickers usually dig a nest cavity in a dead or diseased tree. Often the chosen trees are infected with heart rot fungus, which softens the inside of the tree and makes it easier to excavate. The nest cavities are usually 5 to 8 meters (16 to 26 ft.) off the ground, but I have found some less than a meter (3 ft.) high.

The northern flicker lays an average of six white eggs. In these birds, and many others, the "feel" of the eggs against the female's belly seems to influence the size of her clutch, and she may continue to lay eggs until it feels right. One mother flicker laid 71 eggs in 73 days when an inquisitive researcher removed the eggs as quickly as they were laid.

Chick rearing is a family affair. Both parents incubate the eggs, brood and feed the chicks, and carry away the numerous fecal sacs produced by the nestlings. Young flickers fledge and leave the nest when they are around four weeks old.

The moustache color and red patch on ❯ its nape identifies this flicker as a male yellow-shafted variation.

WESTERN AND EASTERN KINGBIRDS

Colaptes auratus

Family Details

Tyrant Flycatcher Family (Tyrannidae), 400 species worldwide, 6 prairie species

This family of New World flycatchers is one of the largest bird families on Earth and the most numerous of all in the American tropics. In most species the sexes are similar in appearance and are drably feathered in grays, browns, olive-greens, white, and pale yellow. Many flycatchers look very similar, and it's their distinctive vocalizations that differentiate them best.

The common name for their family, flycatcher, describes their frequent foraging method, which is to sit quietly and attentively wait for an insect to go past, then rapidly fly out and capture it on the wing. Most flycatchers have long bristles around the corners of their mouth that act like a net to increase the sensitivity and effectiveness of their capture technique.

Field Identification

The pale gray head, back, and upper breast and pale yellow belly of the western kingbird easily distinguish it from the less colorful eastern kingbird. The latter has a black head, dark gray back, and conspicuous white throat, breast, and belly. The tail pattern can also be used to differentiate the two species. The eastern kingbird has a prominent white-tipped tail whereas the tail on the western kingbird is black with white outer edges. All species in the genus Tyrannus have an orange or red stripe down the middle of their crown, but this is usually hidden and only visible during displays.

Where to Find

Kingbirds usually perch boldly out in the open on fences, power lines, and shrubbery in lightly wooded areas and adjacent to open fields, meadows, and roadsides.

Wintering Grounds

The western kingbird winters along the Pacific slope of southern Mexico and Central America, whereas the eastern kingbird migrates to South America, traveling as far as northern Argentina. Both species return to the prairies around the third week of May and stay until the end of August.

Diet and Feeding Habits

Insects comprise roughly 90 percent of the diet of both species and include honeybees, wasps, grasshoppers, beetles, dragonflies, and damselflies. Both also occasionally eat berries and fruit. As is typical of many flycatchers, kingbirds forage mostly by watching from a perch and then flying out to catch their prey on the wing. They may also hover in place while plucking spiders, leafhoppers, and caterpillars from foliage or the ground. Small prey are eaten while in flight, but larger insects are taken to a nearby perch, beaten until motionless, and then swallowed whole. After short foraging flights, they often return to the same perch.

The eastern kingbird produces a high-pitched, buzzing call, sometimes compared to the sound of an electric fence.

Breeding Biology

Both kingbirds are highly territorial and aggressively chase away intruders. Pairs build a nest of twigs and grasses lined with plant down, feathers, and other fibrous material in a deciduous tree or large shrub, roughly 3 to 10 meters (10 to 33 ft.) off the ground. Their three to five white eggs are heavily marked with brown and incubated for approximately two weeks. The female eastern kingbird does all of the incubation, and the male stands guard when she leaves the nest periodically during the day to forage. It's a different story with western kingbirds as both the male and the female participate in incubation. In both species, the parents feed the chicks for two to three weeks until they eventually fledge. After leaving the nest, fledglings depend upon their parents for food for two to three weeks.

A pair of protective western kingbirds ❯ ferociously attack a red-tailed hawk that happened to trespass on the birds' nesting territory. Photo © Jon Groves

→ **Trivia Tidbit**

The generic name for the kingbirds is Tyrannus, which is derived from Latin meaning "tyrant" and aptly describes their behavior toward potential nest predators. Both male and female kingbirds aggressively attack and pester any crow, raven, magpie, blue jay, kestrel, or hawk that has the temerity to enter their territory during the breeding season. They may even alight on the back of their victims and pull out a feather or two. Unsuspecting blue jays have been knocked out of trees or driven to hide under bushes. Kingbirds are most belligerent when a pair is incubating or feeding young in the nest. Overall, eastern kingbirds have declined by 49 percent since breeding surveys began in 1966.

‹ Male and female western kingbirds look alike.

LOGGERHEAD SHRIKE *Lanius ludovicianus*

Family Details

Shrike Family (Laniidae), 30 species worldwide, 2 prairie species

Shrikes are songbirds that warble and whistle, but they differ from other songsters in one important way: they are predators with a taste for blood. Most shrikes are no larger than a robin, yet they hunt warblers, sparrows, bluebirds, and swallows and capture them in midair. The predatory shrikes also prey on young ground squirrels, voles, mice, frogs, lizards—even small, venomous rattlesnakes.

Shrikes are diurnal hunters with vision much better than humans. Their eyesight may be as good as that of sharp-eyed hawks and falcons. Raptor biologist Dr. Tom Cade had a pet northern shrike. The bird could spot a flying bumblebee 100 meters (328 ft.) away. At that distance the bee was invisible to Cade with his naked eyes, but he could clearly see the insect with seven-power binoculars.

A mouse or a sparrow may be half the size of a shrike, so it would seem that the bird may sometimes tackle prey larger than it can handle. Not likely. A shrike has strong jaw muscles and its hooked upper bill has a special wedge-shaped projection called a tomial tooth on each side just behind the tip. The tomial teeth, also found in falcons, are used by the shrike when it bites its victims on the neck to kill them.

⟨ A male loggerhead shrike retrieves a dead deer mouse it had previously cached in the larder of its territory.

Field Identification

The loggerhead shrike is a gray and white, robin-sized bird with a distinctive black mask and bill and black tail. In flight, the shrike has black wings with a conspicuous white patch near the tips.

Where to Find

The shrike favors open pasturelands with scattered trees and shrubs. These birds frequently perch on fence posts and telephone lines and are often seen along roadsides. The prairie population has been declining for the last 40 years because of poisoning from pesticides and the loss of shelterbelts, hedgerows, willow clumps, and trees to agriculture. It is currently listed as threatened by the Committee on the Status of Endangered Wildlife in Canada (COSEWIC). In a 2014 status report annual declines between 1970 and 2009 were estimated to be 1.2 percent for Alberta, 4.8 percent for Saskatchewan, and 2.2 percent for Manitoba.

Wintering Grounds

Loggerhead shrikes from the northern prairies winter in Mexico and the southern United States.

Diet and Feeding Habits

In some areas, grasshoppers constitute 75 percent of a shrike's diet. The birds also eat beetles, wasps, bumblebees, butterflies, and spiders. Even though insects can be an important food for these birds, they have earned their reputation as rapacious predators because they hunt and kill anything that flutters, scampers, or scurries, including small rodents and many kinds of prairie songbirds.

The shrike, like many falcons, hawks, and eagles, hunts from a perch and captures its victims by a surprise attack from above. If the intended target escapes into a bush or long grass, the shrike does not abandon the chase; it simply jumps and hops about to flush its quarry into flight, where it can again be attacked.

Breeding Biology

Shrikes return to the prairies in early May. The birds are fiercely territorial and aggressively defend a small nesting territory. The scientific name for the loggerhead shrike is *Lanius ludocianus*, which means the "butcher from Louisiana." The Louisiana portion of the name reflects the location of the first specimen described by science, but why is the bird called a butcher? It turns out that male shrikes commonly impale multiple prey items in the same bush or along the same stretch of barbed wire so that the area resembles a butcher shop. In one study, a researcher found a shrike larder with 28 different prey items in it. The researcher emptied the larder and watched to see what the shrike would do. In two days, the larder had been restocked with 26 items. The size of a larder is a display of wealth and skill. A well-stocked larder advertises not only the quality of a male shrike's territory but also his proficiency as a hunter and provider, and, not surprisingly, these attributes are attractive to female shrikes looking for a mate.

The loggerhead shrike commonly builds its nest in thick thorny shrubbery, such as buffaloberry and hawthorn. The female incubates alone and is fed by her mate for the 14 to 16 days it takes the eggs to hatch. The young fledge when they are around 17 days old. The parents continue to attack predators, such as bullsnakes, magpies, and crows in defense of their offspring until the young are six weeks old and can fly well and feed themselves.

→ Trivia Tidbit

The northern shrike (*Lanius excubitor*) is the other species of shrike found in the prairies. It typically nests in the boundary areas between the northern boreal forests and the Arctic tundra and migrates south into the prairies in winter. Its hunting habits in the prairies are very similar to those of the loggerhead shrike, although it preys largely on songbirds and small mammals. Its markings are very similar to those of the loggerhead shrike except that it is slightly larger, paler, and has a more strongly hooked bill.

This pair of northern shrikes was ›
nesting in a clump of willows in
an area of Alaskan tundra.

BLUE JAY *Cyanocitta cristata*

Family Details

Crow, Jay, and Magpie Family (Corvidae) 118 species worldwide, 4 prairie species

This family of medium- to large-sized birds includes the bird brains, tricksters, and mimics of the avian world. They are among the most intelligent of birds, and many have phenomenal memories. A Clark's nutcracker, for example, may hide pine seeds in 2,000 different sites in preparation for winter. Displaying a remarkable spatial memory, the nutcracker can then recall the multitude of locations for up to eight months afterward.

Most of these birds are year-round residents and display great adaptability, especially in their diets. They all have a sturdy, all-purpose bill that enables them to scavenge roadkills and the frozen carcasses of winter-killed animals; rob birds' nests; prey on frogs, snakes, and rodents; pluck berries from bushes; and pick ants and beetles from the ground.

The family members, collectively called corvids, generally have a loud, harsh voice, and their repertoire includes caws, croaks, squawks, and whistles. No one would confuse the noisy call of a corvid with the fluid music of a thrush or a warbler. Even so, the corvids are classified as songbirds, making the common raven the largest songbird in the world.

The blue jay's aptly chosen scientific > name, *Cyanocitta cristata*, means the dark blue, crested bird. Photo © Ken Crebbin

Field Identification

The blue jay is a robin-sized bird, bright blue above and smoky gray underneath. It has a prominent blue crest and a large band of white on its folded wings.

Where to Find

The jay is a year-round resident in woodlands throughout the prairies, but it is most visible in winter when it forages around farms and suburban gardens and parks.

Wintering Grounds

The bright azure plumage of the blue jay is a welcome flush of color on a gray winter day. It is a regular winter patron at bird feeders. A band of these loquacious corvids will drive all other birds away and control the feeder until they have eaten their fill of suet and seeds.

Diet and Feeding Habits

The blue jay, in common with most corvids, has a varied diet. It eats berries, seeds, acorns, beetles, grasshoppers, tent caterpillars, spiders, frogs, and salamanders. A notorious nest-robber, it was immortalized in a painting by the famous bird artist John James Audubon. Audubon wrote: "It [blue jay] imitates the cry of the sparrow hawk so perfectly that the little birds in the neighborhood hurry into thick coverts, to avoid what they believe to be the attack of that marauder. It robs every nest it can find, sucks the eggs like the crow, or tears to pieces and devours the young birds." The jay is a skilled mimic and can also imitate the calls of the red-tailed hawk, the gray catbird, black-capped chickadee, Baltimore oriole, the American goldfinch, and others. It is still a mystery why the jay imitates so many birds.

The blue jay includes ants in its diet, but sometimes the bird uses the insects for something other than food. "Anting" is the preening behavior in which birds anoint their feathers with crushed or live ants. This unusual behavior has been described in nearly 200 species of birds worldwide. Biologists speculate that the acrid formic acid secreted by ants, when wiped through a bird's feathers, may kill or discourage fleas, lice, mites, and other external parasites.

Breeding Biology

The blue jay builds a cup nest of twigs, bark, grass stems, lichens, paper, and feathers in the crotch of a tree, usually 3 to 4 meters (10 to 13 ft.) above the ground. The birds lay four or five pale green eggs spotted with dark brown. The eggs are incubated by the female, but both parents aggressively defend the nest by dive-bombing and pecking intruders. House cats, dogs, and gray squirrels are common targets for their attacks. Anyone who has been scolded by a pair of angry blue jays knows that the noise alone is enough to drive you away. Young jays leave the nest when they are about three weeks old, and the parents continue to feed them for several weeks afterward.

A blue jay will cache seeds to retrieve later, ❯ making multiple trips to a feeder to gather food and store it in a hidden location as far as a kilometer or more away.

BLACK-BILLED MAGPIE *Pica hudsonia*

Family Details

Crow, Jay, and Magpie Family (Corvidae) 118 species worldwide, 4 prairie species

See Blue Jay for a general discussion of the Crow, Jay, and Magpie Family.

Field Identification

The black-billed magpie is a crow-sized bird that is easily identified by its conspicuous black-and-white plumage and long tail. In the right light, the magpie's wings and tail shine iridescent greenish blue making it a very beautiful bird indeed.

Where to Find

The magpie is common in suburban and farming areas throughout the prairies but rarely seen in native grasslands.

Wintering Grounds

The magpie is a year-round resident of the prairies. In winter, the birds do not defend a territory, and travel widely over their home range in loose flocks of a dozen members or more. At night, 100 magpies may roost together in a cluster of trees or bushes.

Diet and Feeding Habits

Typically, the magpie feeds on the ground, hopping or walking with its long handsome tail gracefully angled upwards. This foraging bird flicks litter with its bill, turns over dried cow pies, and chases escaping insects on foot. Magpies eat mostly beetles, wasps, ants, and caterpillars. Its appetite for cutworms, wireworms, grasshoppers, and other insects harmful to crops should make these birds popular with any farmer or rancher. Still, in some rural areas, the magpie is hated and persecuted.

After living on the prairies for 40 years, I've heard all the horror stories about magpies. How they supposedly peck out the eyes of sleeping lambs and calves and eat the kidneys of live sheep by clinging tenaciously to the animals' backs. I've never seen the birds do these things nor have any of the people who enthusiastically tell me these stories, but the tales get repeated nevertheless. With each new telling the yarn gets embellished and magpies get maligned and shot. Certainly, magpies do feed on carrion and winter-killed livestock, and the eyes of dead animals are often the first places they attack because they are easiest to eat. It's laughable, however, to believe that a sheep, no matter how dull-witted, would stand still and let its kidneys be eaten or that a calf or lamb would not awaken when it was pecked in the eye by a magpie.

Breeding Biology

The black-billed magpie stays with the same partner for many years, often until one of them dies. The faithful pair probably builds the most distinctive nest of any prairie bird. The structure is a large, bulky, globular mass of thorny sticks up to 8 meters (26 ft.) off the ground. The woven jumble may be more than a meter (3 ft.) in diameter and take two months to complete. Two or three entrances lead inside, where the birds build a solid nest cup of mud, rootlets, grass stems, and wild animal hair in which to lay their eggs.

Magpies nest in small loose colonies, often in the trees or bushes of a shelterbelt, a fence row, or a river valley. The sturdy nests are often refurbished and used for more than one season. Old abandoned nests are recognizable for five or six years and are used by many other prairie birds. Robins, bluebirds, and sparrows, for example, shelter inside them during bad weather, and some kestrels, merlins, long-eared owls, and mourning doves use them to raise their young. The reason why magpies build such large fortified nests in the first place is still unstudied. The nests may moderate extremes of temperature or simply protect the owners, their eggs, and nestlings from predators, such as crows and ravens. The final answer awaits the scrutiny of a curious, bright-eyed graduate student.

The inside of a magpie nest can get pretty cramped and crowded. A pair may raise five to nine chicks, and they cluster inside the family fortress of sticks until they are almost a month old. By then there is barely room for a bird to blink. Once the youngsters escape to the outside world, they shadow their parents, scrounging and begging for another month until the adults finally refuse to feed them another morsel.

After delivering food to its three chicks, ❯
a mother horned lark removes a fecal sac
from one of them to keep the nest clean.

HORNED LARK *Eremophila alpestris*

Family Details

Lark Family (Alaudidae), 92 species worldwide, 1 prairie species

The larks are small songbirds that live in open grassy plains, deserts, and fields. They do most of their living on the ground, relying on their brown streaky plumage to blend in with the grass, as they feed on insects and seeds. They also court and mate on the ground, with chittering, fluttering, and waving of tails; and nest there, in hidden cups of grass, fur, and feathers. It's when a lark sings that it finally leaves the ground, transforming itself from ordinary to outstanding. Most larks live where there are no trees on which to perch, so they sing on the wing, often high in the sky, and pour out their passion with elaborate, wild music.

In many groups of birds, the voice box, called the syrinx, is controlled by a single pair of muscles. In larks, and other songbirds, five to eight pairs of muscles control the syrinx and produce songs that are complex and beautiful. Each side of the syrinx, in fact, works independently, so a songbird can literally sing a duet with itself.

Field Identification

The horned lark is a small, brown bird with a white belly, black bib and eye line, and small feathered ear tufts that can be raised or lowered. In flight, the bird has a dark tail with white outer feathers. Females are duller in color than males and have less prominent ear tufts.

Where to Find

The horned lark lives in Eurasia as well as North America. It is a lover of open country and big skies and avoids forests. In the prairies, the lark is found in short and mixed grasslands, meadows, and bare fields.

Wintering Grounds

The horned lark is a year-round resident throughout much of its range in the prairies. However, birds in the extreme northern prairies of Canada migrate short distances south. They frequently mix with migratory snow buntings and Lapland longspurs and may wander widely in large nomadic flocks of several hundred birds. Horned larks are one of the first migrants to return to the prairies in spring, often arriving in February.

Diet and Feeding Habits

For most of the year, the lark is a seed eater that feeds on the ground. It likes bare soil and short grasses where it can find its food more easily, and where it has a clear view of the surroundings to watch for predators. In winter, it is frequently seen feeding in fields and flying from one snow-free patch to the next. During the breeding season, when the adults are feeding young, the larks' diet switches to beetles, grasshoppers, and caterpillars.

Breeding Biology

In 1927, ornithologist George Sutton described the voice of the horned lark as "a sweet and delicate tinkling." The horned lark is an early riser, and male songsters usually start to serenade the morning earlier than other prairie birds. Commonly, they begin more than an hour and a half before sunrise and end their recital soon after the sun comes up. They start to sing again several hours before sunset. When a lark sings from the ground, the macho male likes to be elevated, even if that only means standing on the summit of a dried cow patty.

Males also sing on the wing. First, they rapidly and quietly climb to a height of 100 to 250 meters (325 to 820 ft.), then, with their wings and tail spread, they glide and sing. In early spring, when the prairie seems desolate, the delicate music of the lark never fails to brighten my spirits. Such song flights may last up to eight minutes.

The horned lark lays two to five eggs in a hollow cup of feathers and grass on the ground. The female alone incubates the eggs, and the newly hatched nestlings are all mouths and appetites. The insides of their mouths are a vibrant yellow-orange marked with five black spots. The color and spot pattern stimulate the parents to bring food to their chicks and also serve as a "feeding target." In other groups of songbirds, the spot pattern is different for closely related species, and parents will only feed chicks with the unique spot pattern for their own species.

Young horned larks leave the nest when they are about 10 days old and scatter nearby. Separated like this, the chicks are less vulnerable to predators. By four weeks of age, the young larks can fly well and feed themselves.

BARN SWALLOW *Hirundo rustica*

Family Details

Swallow and Martin Family (Hirundinidae), 84 species worldwide, 7 prairie species

This popular and well-known group of small birds are skilled and graceful fliers. Their long, pointed wings give them speed and agility to catch insects in flight. Author John Terres wrote, "... in darting flight, [swallows] hold their tiny but wide-gaping mouths fully open to scoop hundreds of flying insects out of the air." Swallows have small feet and very short legs, and they dislike landing in the thick foliage of trees, so will often perch on wire fences and telephone lines.

Some swallows thrive well around humans, and in North America a number of species commonly nest on buildings and bridges. When I lived in California briefly in the early 1980s, my wife and I went to the famous mission at San Juan Capistrano to witness the annual return of the cliff swallows. Apparently, the swallows first nested on the mission in 1776, and the legend claims that the punctual swallows returned every year after that on March 19. Aubrey and I were on time, but the swallows were not, and we left before the birds finally arrived. Naturally, the cliff swallows of Capistrano are subject to weather delays, as they are everywhere else in the world.

(opposite) This barn swallow was collecting ❭ soft mud from the edge of a puddle that had formed after an overnight rainstorm.

Abandoned rural buildings with their ❭ windows missing are a popular location for barn swallows to nest on the prairies.

Field Identification

The long, deeply forked tail of the barn swallow is the best way to identify this handsome bird. It is iridescent blue on top, bright cinnamon underneath, and has a rusty forehead and throat, making it the most colorful of the prairie swallows.

Where to Find

The barn swallow is common throughout the prairies, frequently nesting around buildings in rural and suburban areas.

Wintering Grounds

The barn swallow winters in southern Mexico, Central America, and the northern parts of South America. During migration it travels during the day in flocks that forage along the way. Among prairie swallow species, the barn swallow is usually the last to leave on its autumn migration, sometimes remaining until the end of September. It returns again in spring by early May.

Diet and Feeding Habits

The agile barn swallow catches flying insects with the aerial agility common to all swallows. It hunts over fields, meadows, sloughs, and marshes. I've seen these delightful swallows follow a farmer cutting hay to catch insects frightened into flight by the machinery. The barn swallow also bathes and drinks on the wing, skimming the surface of the water. It frequently picks up grit or small pebbles, possibly to aid digestion of insects or for its calcium needs.

Breeding Biology

Truthful advertising has always been the best way for a male bird to broadcast his attributes to potential female mates. In the barn swallow, the male's long forked tail is his most important ornament. In these birds, males infested with blood-sucking mites weigh less, have shorter tails, and produce fewer young than do healthy males. Females can detect the slight differences in tail length and use this information to select a mate. Infected male swallows also seem to recognize the superior quality and parenting ability of their longer-tailed male rivals. As a result, they sneak copulations with the female partners of these birds more often than they do with females paired with less healthy mates. Even though this behavior is instinctual, the logic in the strategy is clear. If you are a male, infested with parasites and unable to attract a mate, you can still perpetuate your genes by having a healthy male unknowingly raise your offspring.

Barn swallows nest in small colonies that may contain several dozen pairs. Both partners build the cup-shaped nest using mud, grass stems, hair, and feathers, and cement it to the top of a beam or ledge or plaster it against a vertical wall. The birds lay four or five glossy white eggs speckled with chocolate brown spots. Both parents incubate the eggs and feed the hungry hatchlings. The young swallows can fly by the time they are three weeks old, but for several days afterward they may return at night to the familiar security of the nest to roost. The parents continue to feed the young on the wing for a week or so after they fledge.

TREE SWALLOW *Tachycineta bicolor*

Family Details

Swallow and Martin Family (Hirundinidae), 84 species worldwide, 7 prairie species

See Barn Swallow for a general discussion of the Swallow and Martin Family.

Field Identification

The tree swallow is a small acrobatic bird with long, pointed wings and a notched tail. The bird is an iridescent greenish blue above and white underneath.

Where to Find

This swallow is relatively easy to find in the prairies. Look near fields, native grasslands, and the margins of sloughs, marshes, and lakes. Conservation groups in many areas have erected nest boxes along fence lines for thousands of kilometers. As a result, tree swallows are more common in the prairies than they would normally be.

‹ *(left)* When swallows mate, the coupling lasts just a few seconds. *(top & bottom)* This swallow had found a molted goose feather and eventually added it to the other waterfowl feathers collected to line its nest.

Wintering Grounds

Tree swallows leave the prairies in August and migrate to the Gulf Coast of the southeastern United States, Mexico, and Central America. They return in April, much earlier than other prairie swallows. Their unique ability to digest seeds and fruit allows them to return early when cool weather may still keep their usual insect prey grounded and hard to find.

Diet and Feeding Habits

The tree swallow hunts insects on the wing using steep climbs, dives, and abrupt turns. It commonly forages over fields, cattail marshes, and open water. The agile swallow can swoop down and pluck prey from the surface of the water, and it does this to catch mayflies, caddisflies, and stoneflies. The birds also drink on the wing, gliding over the surface and slicing the water briefly with their open beak.

Breeding Biology

The tree swallow nests in old woodpecker holes or natural cavities in a tree. The competition for such nest sites, and the shortage of them, has influenced the swallows' breeding behavior more than any other factor. The birds' early arrival in spring lets them claim a nest site as soon as possible, and, once they do, they defend it with surprising aggression. The pretty little tree swallow becomes a fierce tiger in the sky, and both sexes will fight to defend their home. Rival swallows will viciously peck each other's head and body in aerial combat, in skirmishes on the ground, in the confinement of a nest cavity, and even in the water. Losers may pay with their life. The competition for nest sites doesn't end there. A homeless female swallow may enter an occupied nest and kill the nestlings, speeding up the desertion of the nest by the resident pair.

Tree swallows also fight with other species for nest cavities. House sparrows will kill adult swallows inside a cavity and then build their own nest on top of the carcass. House-hunting wrens will sneak into a swallow nest and puncture the eggs or peck the nestlings to death. The swallows, in turn, may kill both eastern and mountain bluebirds if they corner them in a cavity. When nest sites are scarce, the stakes are high, and the drive to reproduce forces many birds to battle with their lives.

Tree swallows usually raise four to six chicks. Both parents forage for the young, and a pair of adults may make 20 feeding trips in an hour. The fledglings leave the nest cavity in late May and early June when they are just 18 to 22 days old. The parents feed them for another week or so after that while the young swallows hone their flying and hunting skills.

CLIFF SWALLOW *Hirundo pyrrhonota*

Family Details

Swallow and Martin Family (Hirundinidae), 84 species worldwide, 7 prairie species

See Barn Swallow for a general discussion of the Swallow and Martin Family.

Field Identification

The cliff swallow has a dark back, a white breast and belly, and a black throat. In flight, you can tell it apart from other prairie swallows by its square tail and reddish rump.

Where to Find

The cliff swallow originally nested exclusively on cliff faces in the western mountains. Beginning in the mid-1800s, the swallow gradually expanded its range eastward across the Great Plains into the eastern third of the continent, using buildings, bridges, and highway culverts as new nest sites. The adaptable swallow is now widespread throughout the prairies.

Wintering Grounds

Cliff swallows leave the prairies soon after their chicks fledge. The migration begins in late July, and most are gone by the middle of August. They winter in the marshes and grasslands of Brazil, Paraguay, and Argentina. More than 50,000 swallows roosted in one wetland in northern Argentina. The swallows return to their prairie breeding grounds early in May.

Diet and Feeding Habits

This swallow feeds mainly on flying insects. The birds often forage in groups, sometimes numbering several hundred individuals. The gregarious swallows target the mating swarms of different flies and midges and also take insects that get carried aloft in thermals. Because these swarms of prey are patchy, an individual swallow benefits by hunting in a group and watching the success of its companions. Cliff swallows are the most social swallow in the world and their large nesting colonies function like "information centers." A hungry swallow can watch its neighbors when they bring food to their chicks and follow one of them when it leaves on its next feeding trip. Information sharing, of course, is unintentional, but it benefits every individual in the colony. In the end, swallows that nest in large colonies forage more efficiently and deliver more food to their chicks than those in small colonies.

Breeding Biology

The cliff swallow builds a gourd-shaped nest of mud about the size of a cantaloupe and attaches it to the vertical face of a cliff, building, or bridge. Several thousand pairs may nest together in a single large colony. When the first swallows return in spring, they may claim an existing nest from the previous season. The most desirable nests are those that are not infested by blood-sucking parasites and those located in the center of the colony. Mud nests on the edge of a colony are more vulnerable to predators, especially bullsnakes, which prey on eggs and nestlings and occasionally ambush an adult. In a three-day period, during a study in Nebraska, one bullsnake pillaged dozens of nests and ate 150 eggs.

Cliff swallows fight for the best nests, pecking and tearing at each other with their beaks and beating each other with their wings. When all the old nests are taken, a pair will build a new one. The average mud nest consists of between 900 and 1,200 mud pellets, and it takes the owners a week or two to construct, less time if they share a wall with a neighbor.

The dense colonies in which these swallows nest has led to a couple of interesting behavioral traits; many of the swallows are nest parasites and egg-smashers. In one study, up to 43 percent of nests contained at least one egg that did not belong to the nest owners. This happens in a couple of ways. First, a bird may enter a neighbor's nest and toss out an unguarded egg. Later, the parasite lays a replacement egg in the nest or takes an egg from its own nest, carries it in its beak, and adds it to the neighbor's clutch. Cliff swallows cannot recognize their own eggs and they will incubate any egg they find in their nest.

After all the deceptions, each nesting pair usually hatches three chicks and feeds them for three weeks until they fledge and leave the nest. The parents continue to feed the young by passing them food in flight for another four or five days, after which the young are left to fend for themselves.

BLACK-CAPPED CHICKADEE *Poecile atricapillus*

Family Details

Titmouse Family (Paridae), 54 species worldwide, 2 prairie species

The titmice are small, tame woodland songbirds. Most live in the Northern Hemisphere where they are year-round residents of temperate and boreal forests, and as a result must endure months of winter cold when food is hard to find. One way they survive such harsh environments is to store surplus food, hiding it in under bits of bark, in knotholes, in the broken ends of twigs, and in tufts of conifer needles, retrieving it later when they are hungry. Titmice in Norway, for example, may store between 50,000 and 80,000 spruce seeds each autumn.

Titmice use other ways to survive severe winter conditions. These energetic little birds are literally balls of fluff, and their plumage is much denser than that of other small songbirds. During the coldest weather, they will roost in small tree cavities or holes in the snow where their body heat warms the air around them and helps them to burn less energy. Many titmice, especially chickadees, chill out at night, and let their body temperatures drop 10 to 12°C (18 to 22F°) below their normal daytime temperature of 40°C (104°F). The cooling can yield an energy savings of up to 23 percent and may mean the difference between surviving a frigid night or succumbing to the cold.

Field Identification

The chickadee is a small, active bird with a black cap and bib and white cheeks. In late winter, the distinctive fee-bee call of the chickadee may be the only bird song to interrupt the quiet cold of the prairie woods.

Where to Find

The black-capped chickadee is a common resident of wooded prairie coulees and river valleys, especially where there are groves of aspens.

Wintering Grounds

In winter, chickadees sometimes form temporary flocks with other resident birds. For example, half a dozen chickadees may travel with one or two downy woodpeckers, a red-breasted nuthatch, a white-breasted nuthatch, and a few kinglets and brown creepers. These "mixed feeding flocks" benefit the individuals in a number of ways. In such flocks, there are more eyes to detect danger, and the flight of a large group of birds is more likely to confuse a predator and foil its attack. As well, when different species of birds forage close together in a flock they can learn about new food sources from each other. For example, chickadees will sometimes visit a site where a woodpecker was hammering to investigate what the bird found to eat.

Diet and Feeding Habit

The black-capped chickadee finds most of its food in three ways. More than half the time, the bird simply hops along small branches searching the bark and leaves for scale insects, plant lice, and beetles. Less often it uses its strong legs to hang upside down like an acrobat on the underside of branches so it can locate hidden insects. Finally, it can hover, and pluck caterpillars from the outermost leaves.

Chickadees will also eat the hairy caterpillars of the gypsy moth and the tent caterpillar moth, both of which are often rejected by other insectivorous birds. Veteran chickadee researcher Dr. Susan Smith has seen black-capped chickadees repeatedly tearing open the silken nests of tent caterpillars to feed on the juicy grubs.

The autumn and winter diet of the chickadee contains much less animal food. In these seasons of austerity, the birds commonly eat berries and seeds, especially the seeds of coniferous trees. They also scour the bark of trees and bushes to search for dormant insect eggs and hibernating spiders.

Breeding Biology

The chickadee nests in a tree cavity, which the pair excavates in the rotten wood of a limb, stump, or knothole. The inside of the cavity is well lined with fur, feathers, fine strips of bark, moss, and plant down. In early May, the female lays six to nine speckled eggs and incubates them alone while her mate continues to feed her. The young hatchlings must be brooded continuously by the female until they are 12 days old and feathered enough to keep themselves warm. During this time, the "submissive" male continues to feed his "dominant" mate as well as the young. The chicks fledge a few days later and the family travels together for two to four weeks afterward. Family breakup is abrupt, and all the youngsters disperse within one or two days.

❮ The black-capped chickadee, literally a ball of fluff, relies on its thick plumage to shield it from the cold.

The English poet and painter William ❯
Blake wrote, "He who shall hurt the littie
wren, shall never be loved by men."

HOUSE WREN *Troglodytes aedon*

Family Details

Wren Family (Troglodytidae), 76 species worldwide, 4 prairie species

The wrens are a family of small chunky birds with slender pointed bills and up-tilted tails. The majority of these energetic little birds live in the tropics of Central and South America. The scientific name for the group, Troglodytidae, is derived from the Greek for cave dweller or one who lives in dark secret places. The name is well chosen since many wrens inhabit dense underbrush and reedy marshes where they hop and flit around, stealthily peer out, and then disappear again into the shadows.

Most wrens are plain brownish in color. This is not surprising, since bright colorful plumage would be wasted in the dim, shadowed world in which these birds live. Rather than use conspicuous plumage to signal each other and communicate, rival wrens use their voices, and many of them are superb singers with rich, complicated songs.

One of the most unusual behaviors seen among wrens is the habit that many males have of building "dummy nests." A male may build a dozen or more nests, only one of which will be used by his mate to lay her eggs. Some scientists speculate that the multiple nests may be an anti-predator strategy, the reasoning being that once a nest-robber checks a few nests and finds them empty it will stop looking and leave before it locates the real nest.

Field Identification

The house wren is one of those confusing LBJs (Little Brown Jobs) that exasperate birdwatchers. This brownish wren is smaller than a sparrow and often carries its tail cocked forward over its back. Its call is a delightful bubbling cascade of whistles that is not easily confused with the song of any other prairie bird.

Where to Find

The house wren is found in dense thickets throughout the prairies. This inquisitive little bird readily settles close to humans, and, as its common name suggests, it will nest near houses and buildings if there is thick shrubbery nearby where it can retreat.

Wintering Grounds

This tiny wren, which weighs only 10 to 12 grams (0.4 to 0.5 oz.) when it is fattened up for its autumn migration, flies to the southern United States and Mexico for the winter. Most house wrens leave in August and early September and are back on the prairies by the middle of May.

Diet and Feeding Habits

The house wren may sometimes forage high in the foliage of a tree but most often hunts near the ground in dense shrubbery, exploring every nook and cranny for crickets, beetles, ticks, spiders, plant lice, ants, wasps, and bees. This small pugnacious bird often punctures the eggs or kills the nestlings of bluebirds, tree swallows, and other house wrens. The wren never eats the eggs or chicks of its victims, and its killing instinct apparently is a strategy to lessen competition for nest sites rather than a tactic to obtain food.

Breeding Biology

The male house wren defends a small territory and advertises his ardor by singing loudly and often. The house wren always nests in a cavity, but at times it ends up in some rather unexpected locations. Besides the usual knotholes, old woodpecker holes, rock cavities, and crevices in trunks and broken snags, the wren may also settle inside the dried skull of a cow, in an old boot or shoe, in a flowerpot, or in the tailpipe of an abandoned tractor. Typically, the male builds several "dummy" nests of sticks and twigs and then waits for Lady Wren to make her choice and add the finishing touch: a fine lining of feathers, hair, and plant fibers. A pair of house wrens usually raises six to eight young, and they may set a feeding record doing it. According to author Frank Todd the house wren may feed its young more frequently than any other bird in North America. In Todd's fascinating book *10,001 Titillating Tidbits of Avian Trivia* he writes that one male house wren returned to the nest 1,217 times within a 16.25-hour period—an average of one feeding visit every 47 seconds! The hard work ends when the wrenlets finally leave the nest between 14 and 18 days of age.

MARSH WREN *Cistothorus palustris*

Family Details

Wren Family (Troglodytidae), 76 species worldwide, 4 prairie species

See House Wren for a general discussion of the Wren Family.

Field Identification

This brownish wren has a prominent white eye line and a whitish throat and underparts. The marsh wren lives in bulrushes and cattails, and this habit can be used to distinguish it from all other prairie wrens except possibly the sedge wren, which at times may live in reedy marshes. The sedge wren differs in having buffy underparts and a streaked crown. If you have reached this level of birding skill you don't need me to help you, and I won't say another word.

Where to Find

The wren is found in large cattail marshes and sloughs throughout much of the prairies.

Wintering Grounds

Marsh wrens leave in August to winter in the coastal marshes of the Gulf of Mexico and in fresh and saltwater wetlands throughout Mexico. Most wrens are back on the prairies calling from the cattails by early May.

Diet and Feeding Habits

The marsh wren is a spider's worst nightmare, and these eight-legged wolves are one of the bird's most common foods. The sharp-beaked little wrens also hunt beetles, bees, wasps, bugs, and moths. In their 1997 monograph *Marsh Wren*, authors Drs. Donald Kroodsma and Jared Verner wrote, "Foraging wrens are nearly always on the move, hopping and creeping among the bases of cattail stalks or threading their way through a tangle of fallen bulrush stems."

Breeding Biology

American naturalist and painter John James Audubon thought the marsh wren's rattling call resembled "the grating of a rusty hinge." Only male wrens sing, and these little testosterone-charged songsters can really whistle. In western Nebraska, each male marsh wren sings an average of 211 different songs. Neighboring males commonly engage in vocal duels, imitating each other's songs and trying to outdo one another, and these long-winded singers chatter day and night. In a Manitoba marsh, the wrens called at night, between 1 a.m. and 3 a.m., as often as they did during the day. Calling at night may lessen interference from other marsh-dwelling songbirds.

Male marsh wrens work while they whistle, building half a dozen "dummy" nests for every female partner they have, and some males may eventually mate with two or three partners. In a cattail marsh in Manitoba, 8 percent of the males were bachelors, 44 percent had a single mate, 40 percent were bigamists, and 8 percent were trigamists.

Marsh wrens build globe-shaped nests made of cattails, sedges, and grasses, somewhat smaller than a football and anchored to a dried cluster of cattail stalks. The male adds a lining of plant down inside the nest, and later his female partner adds grasses, rootlets, and fine strips of marsh vegetation to the one she will use.

The marsh wren lays a clutch of four to six pinkish-buff-colored eggs flecked with grayish brown scribbles and spots. The female incubates the eggs alone for 13 days and provides most of the meals for the hatchlings. The male wren may, or may not, help feed the chicks, and this varies among different populations of marsh wrens. In the marshes of New York State, for example, no males fed their offspring, whereas in Manitoba nine out of 65 males brought food to their chicks, but only after the nestlings were eight days old. Despite such poor male participation, male wrens that feed their chicks produce heavier nestlings and fledge more young than do absentee fathers.

At two weeks of age, young marsh wrens drop out of their cattail nests and scurry into cover. The young wrens are fed by one or both parents for a couple of weeks after they leave the nest.

‹ *(opposite)* In a congested cattail marsh, male wrens and females call to indicate their location and alert each other to danger.

The nest of the marsh wren consists mainly › of the soft, fibrous fluff from cattail seed heads lined with fine grasses.

AMERICAN ROBIN *Turdus migratorius*

Family Details

Thrush Family (Turdidae), 165 species worldwide, 6 prairie species

The thrushes are a family of small to medium-sized woodland songbirds. Many of them forage on the ground where they use their strong legs to scratch in the leaf litter for insects and earthworms. A cryptic plumage of gray, brown, and white is common among the thrushes and camouflages them well in the mixture of light and shadow on the forest floor. Some thrushes, however, namely the bluebirds, are brightly colored and forage in the open, where their vibrant plumage flashes in the sunshine.

Thrushes are noted for their beautiful eggs. Among the North American species, almost all of them lay glossy, greenish blue eggs, some of which are accented with rusty speckles and splotches. From a scientific standpoint, it's unclear why the eggs are so brightly colored. Regardless, the blue egg color of one of the thrushes is so striking and distinctive that it is now used as an accepted color standard—robin's egg blue.

Field Identification

The American robin is so familiar to everyone that it hardly needs to be described. The male bird's distinctive rusty chest and belly reminded early British settlers of the English robin (actually an Old World flycatcher) with its reddish face and breast, and the homesick colonists gave it the same name. The male and female American robin are similar except the female's breast color is somewhat duller.

Where to Find

The robin is common in wooded river valleys and coulees throughout the prairies. The bird adapts well to humans and frequently nests in farmyards and suburban gardens and parks.

Wintering Grounds

The American robin winters throughout the southern United States. The few that try to winter on the prairies invariably succumb to the cold. Every year in April, without fail, the local television station announces the first spring sighting of the robin in our area of the prairies. For most viewers, the cheery bird is the surest sign that summer is on the way.

❮ A spring snowstorm can be stressful for a migrating robin, not because of the cold temperatures, but because food may be hard to find.

Diet and Feeding Habits

In typical thrush fashion, the robin often forages on the ground, running for its meals. It hunts in meadows, plowed fields, lawns, and golf courses and searches for wireworms, cutworms, beetles, ants, termites, and grasshoppers. Who has not seen a photograph of a plump-chested robin leaning back, tugging on an earthworm anchored in the soil and stretched to the breaking point? The final score in this familiar contest is always the same: Robins one, Earthworms zero. I always wondered how a robin locates an earthworm in the first place. The bird often tilts its head when it is hunting as if it is listening for prey to reveal itself. Researcher Frank Heppner solved the mystery in an erudite paper entitled "Sensory mechanisms and environmental clues used by the American robin in locating earthworms." Heppner's conclusion was that the robin finds worms in their burrows not by sound but by sight. The bird simply cocks its head to improve its depth perception so that it can strike with greater accuracy.

In autumn, flocks of robins travel together and settle on berry bushes and fruit trees. In the prairies, their favorites include pin cherries, choke cherries, saskatoons, and rose hips, which they devour with equal relish.

Breeding Biology

Everyone wonders if the robins nesting in their yard are the same ones that nested there the year before. A pioneer study done in the 1940s determined that 74 percent of robins returned to within 16 kilometers (10 mi.) of their original homes. Since many robins live to be eight or nine years old, and some 15 years old, the robin nesting in your yard may very well be an old friend.

The female robin is an independent mother who builds the nest and incubates the eggs pretty well on her own. The nest is bulky and cup-shaped, made of coarse grasses, leaves, and rootlets cemented together with mud. It is usually less than 6 meters (20 ft.) off the ground on a ledge or tree limb. The female usually lays four unmarked glossy eggs. Male robins do not feed their mates, so the female must balance her nest duties with the needs of everyday life. As a result, throughout the day, the female incubates in shifts lasting about three-quarters of an hour separated by a 10-minute break during which time she feeds herself, preens, and stretches.

Newly hatched robin chicks are blind and completely helpless. The linings of their mouths are bright lemon yellow and they wave them instinctively any time an adult lands and jars the nest. The male helps his mate feed the chicks. Once they fledge at two weeks of age, he may continue to feed them for another week or 10 days while the female prepares to raise a second clutch of eggs.

This male bluebird is delivering a darkling ❯ beetle (Tenebrionidae) to his chicks.

❮ Both male and female bluebirds adjust the size of the prey they deliver to nestlings based on the gape size of the chicks, bringing smaller items initially and larger ones as the chicks get older.

MOUNTAIN BLUEBIRD *Sialia currucoides*

Family Details

Thrush Family (Turdidae), 165 species worldwide, 6 prairie species
See American Robin for a general discussion of the Thrush Family.

Field Identification

The male is cerulean blue above and pale sky-blue underneath. In flight, no other prairie bird has such brilliant blue wings. The female is much less colorful and has a grayish brown head and body with some blue in her wings, tail, and rump.

Where to Find

The mountain bluebird is a bird of the western prairies where it inhabits badlands, sagebrush flats, grasslands, and the edge of wooded coulees. Nest boxes have encouraged these bold, beautiful birds to settle along roadways throughout the west.

Wintering Grounds

The mountain bluebird is the most migratory of the three species of bluebirds found in North America. Most winter in the southwestern United States or northwestern Mexico. They leave the northern prairies by mid-September but return again toward the end of winter, usually in late March and early April. In most years, the males precede the females by several weeks.

Diet and Feeding Habits

The mountain bluebird is one of the most carnivorous of the thrushes, eating more insects and less fruit than do most of them. Typically, it hunts from an elevated perch or by hovering. When prey is sighted, it quickly flutters to the ground and grabs the hapless victim with its sharp-edged beak. The most common food items include crickets, spiders, grasshoppers, caterpillars, beetles, butterflies, and ants.

Breeding Biology

Male mountain bluebirds are highly aggressive and defend their nest territory with chases and aerial displays in which rival males hover in front of each other, flashing the intense blue in their plumage as they rapidly open and close their wings. If neither opponent is intimidated, hovering rivals may attack each other and grapple in flight. I once caught a male bluebird aggressively pecking its own reflection in the side mirror of my SUV. The pugnacious bluebird returned to battle with his imaginary enemy half a dozen times in 15 minutes, even after I sat in the driver's seat directly beside the mirror.

Despite the vigilance of resident male bluebirds, intruders commonly trespass on their territories, and rival males may try to mate with the owner's partner. To prevent this, male mountain bluebirds guard their mates "jealously" throughout nest building and egg laying, when the female is most fertile. At these times, the male stays very close to his partner and never lets her out of his sight. This, in fact, is the only way the male can be certain that he will be feeding his own offspring rather than those of some dashing outsider.

Mountain bluebirds commonly nest in tree cavities, rock crevices, and bird houses. Such nest cavities are often in short supply and many species compete for them, including northern flickers, house wrens, house sparrows, and European starlings. In many of these house wars, the bluebirds lose and are ousted, their eggs destroyed or nestlings murdered.

A bluebird family consists of five or six young, and the female broods the nestlings almost continuously until they are a week old. The hardworking male feeds both the female and the chicks. After a week, however, both parents bring caterpillars, grasshoppers, and spiders to the young, which grow quickly on this highly nutritious diet. Most bluebird chicks fledge between 18 and 21 days after hatching but continue to depend on their parents to feed them for several weeks afterward.

Two unexpected threats to bluebird nestlings come from insects and mammals. Stinging carpenter ants and blood-sucking blackflies may kill young chicks, and deer mice may take over the family nest, destroying the eggs and nestlings, even killing the adult female.

❮ (opposite) In mountain bluebirds the cycle from eggs to empty nest takes five and a half to six weeks.

This female bluebird has a beak filled ❯ with a field cricket (Gryllidae) and a tiger moth caterpillar (Erebidae)."

EASTERN BLUEBIRD *Sialia sialis*

Family Details

Thrush Family (Turdidae), 165 species worldwide, 6 prairie species

See American Robin for a general discussion of the Thrush Family.

Field Identification

The male eastern bluebird is deep blue above with a rusty throat, breast, and sides. The female is similar but paler. The color in a bird's feathers is produced either by pigments or by the optical effects of light on the microscopic structure of the feather. In the case of bluebirds, the intense blue color is an optical illusion caused by the structure of their feathers.

Where to Find

The eastern bluebird is restricted to the eastern half of the prairies. This handsome songbird prefers forest edges and is seen less often in treeless habitats than is the mountain bluebird. Like all bluebirds, the eastern species often associates with humans and may be found around farmhouses and shelterbelts.

Wintering Grounds

Most eastern bluebirds overwinter in the southeastern United States.

Diet and Feeding Habits

This bluebird commonly hunts in two ways: still-hunting from a perch and hover-hunting. In the former, the bird sits on an elevated perch, often a fence wire or tree branch, waiting patiently for unsuspecting prey to fly, hop, or scuttle by. From its perch, the sharp-eyed bluebird skillfully flies out to catch butterflies, wasps, and bees in midair or dives to the ground to capture grasshoppers, spiders, caterpillars, beetles, ants, centipedes, and millipedes.

Hover-hunting can burn up to eight times more energy than still-hunting so the rewards need to balance the energetic costs. Not surprisingly, bluebirds hover more often when the wind is blowing strongly and there is more lift to the air. The birds also hover-hunt more when they are feeding hungry young. In the latter instance, the added foraging cost is necessary to meet the nutritional needs of their offspring.

The bluebird, in common with most thrushes, adds berries to its diet when the fruit ripens in the late summer and autumn. When berries are plentiful, bluebirds may gather in flocks of 100 or more to feed together.

Breeding Biology

In courtship, the female sits and evaluates, while the male flutters and flashes. Typically, the hopeful male suitor, while singing, fans his azure tail and hovers in front of the perched female. It is likely the female can assess the health and vitality of her prospective mate by the vigor of his hovering and the brilliance of his plumage.

The eastern bluebird is a cavity-nester as are all bluebirds. Old woodpecker holes, crevices in tree trunks, and hollows in stumps and old fence posts are popular natural nest sites. In the last 40 years, many eastern bluebirds have moved into birdhouses built specifically for them along "bluebird trails." Recent innovations in the design of the birdhouses have lessened competition with other cavity-nesters, such as tree swallows, wrens, house sparrows, and starlings, all of whom covet the dry, snug birdhouses.

Potential nest cavities are often scarce, and the male bluebird's territory centers around these valuable sites. Inside the nest cavity, the female weaves a loose cup of grasses, feathers, and animal hair where she lays four to six pale blue, glossy eggs. Incubation and chick rearing take roughly six weeks. During the final week or 10 days, the male may feed the chicks alone while the female re-nests.

→ Trivia Tidbit

The handsome bluebird is an obvious choice as a state bird. Idaho and Nevada use the mountain bluebird as their official avian ambassador, and the eastern bluebird is the state bird of Missouri and New York.

The blue color of the eastern bluebird is ↘ recognizably different than that of the mountain bluebird. The abundance of both species has been greatly increased by committed volunteers who maintain "bluebird trails" — strings of bird houses erected along countless miles of rural highways and country roads.

EUROPEAN STARLING *Sturnus vulgaris*

Family Details

Starling and Myna Family (Sturnidae), 115 species worldwide, 1 introduced prairie species

This is a family of stocky medium-sized birds ranging in length from 15 to 40 centimeters (6 to 16 in.), many of them brightly colored in iridescent greens, blues, and purples. Most starlings and mynas live in the tropics of Africa, Asia, and the South Pacific, and none is native to the Americas. Two introduced species are found in North America, the crested myna and the familiar European starling. The ubiquitous starling was released in New York's Central Park in 1890 and 1891 in a misguided effort to introduce all of the birds mentioned in the writings of William Shakespeare.

The starlings and their relatives are renowned vocal mimics. For centuries, mynas in Asia have been kept as pets because of their ability to mimic human voices. The European starling is also no slouch when it comes to mimicry. Individual starlings may imitate the calls of 20 different bird species, the most common being the American robin, killdeer, red-winged blackbird, meadowlark, northern flicker, and American crow. Ornithologists are uncertain of the biological purpose of mimicry, but it may be one way for a bird to enlarge its song repertoire, which is often a measure of the quality of a male suitor. In some species, mating success increases with increased repertoire size, and this may be ample reason for a starling to imitate all its neighbors.

Field Identification

The European starling is a year-round resident of the prairies. In late summer, autumn, and winter, the bird is black, finely speckled with white, with a black beak. In the breeding season, the speckles disappear and the starling is glossy black, all over, with green and purple iridescent highlights, and its beak turns yellow. Unlike most birds, which acquire their breeding plumage by replacing their feathers in a late winter molt, the starling loses its speckles by abrasion, gradually wearing away the white tips on its feathers.

Where to Find

A hundred starlings were released into New York City in the late 1890s, and today they number over 200 million. These tough adaptable birds were first sighted in prairie Alberta in 1934, and by 1970 they were breeding in Alaska. Starlings now occur continent-wide south of the treeline. Researcher Dr. Paul Cabe believes "[Starlings] are arguably the most successful avian intruder to the continent." The European starling thrives especially well in agricultural and urban areas throughout the prairies.

Wintering Grounds

Starlings winter on the prairies. At the end of the breeding season, the birds gradually gather in flocks and roost together at night. The roosting flocks are largest in winter, and in some areas of the continent may contain more than a million birds.

Diet and Feeding Habits

Everyone has seen these chunky, square-tailed birds walking and running on their lawns searching for beetles, flies, caterpillars, grasshoppers, snails, earthworms, and spiders. Although starlings prefer invertebrates when they are available, the versatile birds also eat grain, livestock feed, berries, fruits, and garbage. Their diverse diet partly explains why some people call them "rats with wings."

Breeding Biology

Male starlings usually mate with a single partner, but in some populations they pair with a second female. Second mates receive little help in incubating their eggs or feeding the young, and, as a result, they fledge fewer chicks than primary mates.

Starlings commonly nest in cavities in buildings, in unused woodpecker holes, and in nest boxes. They are surprisingly aggressive in evicting other species from such sites. Flickers, tree swallows, and bluebirds are frequent victims of these nest pirates. Once starlings claim a site, they fill the cavity with an untidy mix of grasses, rootlets, feathers, paper, string, and bits of plastic garbage. The usual clutch is five to seven pale blue eggs, which both parents incubate. The eggs hatch after two weeks, and the young fledge when they are three weeks old. Although the young may follow their parents and beg for food for several weeks afterward, they are rarely fed for more than a few days after they leave the nest.

YELLOW WARBLER *Dendroica petechia*

Family Details

New World Warbler Family (Parulidae), 112 New World species, 27 prairie species

The New World warblers live only in the Americas and are a group of small delicate songbirds that flutter and flit among the leaves of shrubs and trees. They have slender pointed bills that they use to pick insects off vegetation. Half a dozen different warblers may forage in the same tree at the same time. They lessen competition by masterfully partitioning the habitat, feeding at different levels in the tree, and at different distances from the trunk. Most warblers are much smaller than sparrows, and they are often overlooked because of their tiny size and their habit of hunting quietly in the treetops and in shrubbery. On closer inspection, however, the males of many warbler species are colorfully feathered during the breeding season, and, like flowers on the wing, these handsome little birds brighten any spring day.

Field Identification

The yellow warbler is sometimes called the "wild canary" and is the only small all-yellow bird found in the prairies. The male has delicate rusty streaks on its breast and belly. This beautiful little songster might be confused with the similar-sized goldfinch, but the finch has a conspicuous black cap, wings, and tail.

Where to Find

The yellow warbler is one of the most widely distributed warblers in North America and ranges from the Arctic treeline to the Rio Grande in Texas. In the prairies, the warbler is found in thickets of shrubbery along waterways and in moist areas at the edges of woodlands.

Wintering Grounds

The yellow warbler, like all insect-eating songbirds, flees from the prairies in winter as it would quickly succumb to the cold if it were to stay. Many leave in August and migrate to Mexico and Central America, although some may fly as far south as Brazil.

Diet and Feeding Habits

This warbler often hunts close to the ground, searching in shrubbery on the underside of leaves and stems for hiding insects. Although caterpillars may comprise more than two-thirds of its diet, the warbler also eat moths, bark beetles, damselflies, aphids, and grasshoppers. Yellow warblers, along with many other insect-eating songbirds, use leaf damage to focus their foraging efforts to help them locate caterpillars more easily. In this deadly contest of hide-and-seek, many edible caterpillars lessen their chances of being eaten by feeding at night, by trimming the eaten leaves to make them less conspicuous to birds, and by hiding at sites away from the damaged leaves where they are less likely to be found.

⟨ Scientists recognize 35 subspecies of yellow ⟩
warblers in all of the Americas. Aside from
subtle differences in feather pattern, yellow
warblers that live the farthest north are
the largest and those living in the wettest
environments are the darkest.

Breeding Biology

The female yellow warbler is remarkably tame as she builds the family nest over a three- to four-day period, and I once watched one of them at close range in a clump of willows. The nest was just a meter (3 ft.) off the ground and consisted of a compact cup of dry grass stems, plant down, and feathers nestled in a crotch between several branches. Some female warblers also use spider silk or the silken nests of tent caterpillars to bind the nest materials together.

Yellow warblers are usually monogamous, and the female builds her nest in the middle of the defended territory of her sweet-singing mate. The bird typically lays four to five white or light greenish eggs, speckled with dark brown, and she alone incubates the clutch for the 11 days it takes before the family hatches. Young warblers, like many songbird chicks, are ugly little wobbly necked critters with huge red mouths rimmed in bright yellow—a target that is hard to miss for a feeding parent. Both adults feed the hungry chicks, which leave the nest before they are two weeks of age.

The yellow warbler is a frequent victim of the parasitic brown-headed cowbird, which lays its eggs in the nests of other birds and then lets the foster parents raise the young for them. In many cases, when a warbler discovers a cowbird egg in its nest it may desert the nest or simply bury the entire clutch in nest materials, and then lay a replacement clutch on top. Even so, yellow warblers are still the number one songbird chosen by the parasitic cowbirds.

SPOTTED TOWHEE *Pipilo maculatus*

Family Details

Sparrow, Bunting, and Longspur Family (Emberizidae), 49 species, 27 prairie species

This family of songbirds, most of whom are colored in shades of brown, gray, and buff, spend most of their time foraging on the ground where their cryptic plumage camouflages them. The foraging style of many family members includes scratching with both feet simultaneously, descriptively called a hop-scratch. In this they make a short jump forward and then scratch back with both feet at once. They have strong legs with large feet and well-developed claws. All have a short, sturdy, conical bill well-suited to cracking seeds, which is their main diet in winter. In summer they feed largely on insects. Many are known to swallow small bits of gravel that assist the birds' muscular gizzard in grinding and digesting tough-coated seeds.

Outside the breeding season they may form flocks, sometimes mixing with other species.

Field Identification

The towhee is a large sparrow with a long black tail, white undersides, and conspicuous rusty sides. The bird's brilliant red eye stands out in sharp contrast with its all-black head. The white spots on its shoulders and upper back distinguish it from the similar-looking eastern towhee that is found east of the Great Plains. For many years, the two were thought to be variations of a single species but are now recognized as distinct species, although where their ranges overlap the two may sometimes interbreed.

Where to Find

In their 1976 classic *The Birds of Alberta*, Ray and Jim Salt described the favorite haunts of the towhee as "tangles of rose-bush, saskatoon, hawthorn, and willow on the slopes of prairie coulees and dense undergrowth under poplars and cottonwoods along prairie rivers and creeks."

Wintering Grounds

The handsome towhee winters in the southwestern United States, moving southward from the prairies in September and returning again in late April or early May.

Diet and Feeding Habits

The towhee's distinctive scratching behavior displaces leaf litter and loose soil, exposing beetles, crickets, grasshoppers, millipedes, sowbugs, and spiders as well as small seeds. The opportunistic towhee also forages aboveground in shrubs and low trees where it feeds on caterpillars, moths, spiders, and berries.

Breeding Biology

Males aggressively defend a nesting territory, which they advertise by singing, often from an elevated perch at the top of a bush. Trespassing males are chased. When rare fights occur, the combatants may engage in face-to-face grappling, grabbing each other with their claws and using their wings and bill as weapons.

The female builds a deep, open cup nest of leaves, grasses, and twigs lined with fine rootlets in a bush, on or very close to the ground. Her male partner often accompanies her as she collects nest material, presumably to prevent a rival male from mating with her. The pair's clutch of four to five greenish eggs are incubated solely by the female for 12 to 14 days. The well-insulated nest enables her to keep the temperature of her eggs and brooded hatchlings up to 17C° (30F°) warmer than the surrounding air temperature. During incubation, the male occasionally visits the nest to feed his mate, although she frequently leaves for short periods to forage on her own. The blind, nearly naked hatchlings are brooded solely by the female, but both parents feed the chicks until they abandon the nest when they are nine to 11 days old. The nestlings are unable to fly when they first leave the nest, and both parents feed them for another 30 days until they become totally independent.

(left) The long claws on a towhee's feet are ❯ well adapted for scratching in leaf litter.
(right) The songs of male towhees display regional dialects that the young learn when they are nestlings.

CHESTNUT-COLLARED LONGSPUR

Calcarius ornatus

Family Details

Sparrow, Bunting, and Longspur Family (Emberizidae), 49 species, 27 prairie species

See Spotted Towhee for a general discussion of the Sparrow, Bunting, and Longspur Family.

Field Identification

This chunky sparrow frequently walks and runs on the ground. Its common name is derived from the long nail on its hind toe, the function of which is unclear. The large chestnut patch on the male's hindneck combined with his buffy white cheeks and throat distinguish him from all other prairie sparrows. The female is a drab gray-brown overall. When either sex flies, their white outer tail feathers are a conspicuous field sign.

Where to Find

The chestnut-collared longspur is a typical bird of the dry-grass plains of the northern prairies. Before much of the area was plowed for agriculture, the longspur was one of the most common birds in the prairies. Today, it occurs in the few remaining tracts of native grasslands as well as in pasturelands and poor croplands where growth is sparse and short.

Wintering Grounds

Longspurs winter in the southern prairies of the United States and in the Central Plateau of northern Mexico. They migrate south in September and return north again in early April.

Diet and Feeding Habits

Like many sparrows, the longspur feeds heavily on seeds, especially during the winter. During the summer breeding season, however, it hunts beetles, crickets, and grasshoppers, which are high in fat and protein. An invertebrate-rich diet is vital for growing nestlings and comprises the bulk of the food that adults feed to their young. Longspurs are strictly diurnal and generally forage by walking and picking food off the ground. If a grasshopper, moth, or butterfly suddenly takes flight in front of it the bird will try to capture it on the wing. In a Colorado study, such fly-catching behavior occurred in a quarter of successful captures.

Breeding Biology

The male longspur advertises his ownership of a patch of prairie real estate with a melodious song given on the wing or from an elevated perch, such as atop a cluster of sagebrush. The female digs a shallow hollow in the ground, then lines it with a nest of fine grasses, feathers, and hair. The nest is usually located in sparse vegetation near a landmark stone or bush. I've accidentally found two longspur nests, and both were beside an old cow patty hidden under a clump of grass. The female flushed from the nest only when I was less than 1.5 meters (5 ft.) from her, and she then fluttered through the grass with her wings outstretched trying to distract me.

Only the female has an incubation patch—a featherless area on the abdomen used to warm the eggs—so she alone tends her clutch of three to five eggs until they hatch after 10 to 12 days. The parents eat the eggshells or carry them away, sometimes up to 30 meters (98 ft.) from the nest, to lessen the possibility that the hatchlings will be found by a sharp-eyed predator. Both parents feed the chicks, each making five or six feeding trips to the nest per hour. In a Saskatchewan study, popular foods were leafhoppers, grasshoppers, spiders, and caterpillars. The young leave the nest 10 days after hatching and are fed for another two weeks.

The territorial song of the chestnut- › collared longspur is often given on the wing and having a black breast and belly makes the songster more conspicuous against the brightness of the sky.

SNOW BUNTING *Plectrophenax nivalis*

Family Details

Sparrow, Bunting, and Longspur Family (Emberizidae), 49 species, 27 prairie species

See Spotted Towhee for a general discussion of the Sparrow, Bunting, and Longspur Family.

Field Identification

In winter, the male and female look similar with buffy grayish plumage tinged with rust on their shoulders, back, and head. They are easily identified when they fly and reveal the contrasting black and white areas on their wings and tail. Male snow buntings usually migrate north from the prairies before they acquire their distinctive overall black-and-white breeding plumage.

Where to Find

Snow buntings often gather in large flocks in stubble fields in winter, accompanied by Lapland longspurs. Many locals affectionately refer to them as "snowbirds" because when a flock takes flight from a winter field they resemble snowflakes swirling across the prairie.

⟨ (left) On the snow bunting's Arctic nesting grounds the ermine is an ever-present threat to the bird's eggs and hatchlings. (top) On their prairie wintering grounds male and female snow buntings look roughly the same, and only after migrating north do the males (bottom) adopt their crisp black-and-white finery.

Wintering Grounds

The buntings are strictly winter birds that arrive on the prairies in late autumn from their Arctic nesting grounds. They start to leave again in March. Lapland longspurs and horned larks are migrating at the same time, and the three species are frequently found together.

Diet and Feeding Habits

On their prairie wintering grounds the buntings eat mainly weed and grass seeds, but on their Arctic breeding grounds they have a mixed diet of buds, seeds, insects, and spiders. As with many songbirds, the young are fed exclusively with insects and spiders. Studies suggest that snow buntings' plumage is thicker than other similar-sized songbirds, which enables them to withstand lower ambient temperatures without having to increase their food intake—a survival advantage for early spring migrants returning to a snow-covered Arctic.

Breeding Biology

Males arrive on their Arctic breeding grounds up to a month before females. Nests are typically far under boulders or deep in rock crevices or cliff faces. I have found nests in Arctic communities where the birds used old metal pipes, stone foundations, crevices in buildings, even spaces in abandoned snowmobiles. Both sexes inspect potential nest cavities, but only the female builds the nest, which is a thick-walled cup of grasses, feathers, and fur. One old nest I found on Victoria Island, Nunavut, had a thick lining of muskox hair and ptarmigan and snowy owl feathers. Suitable nest cavities may be a limiting factor for breeding, so snow buntings will reuse old nests and add a new lining.

Snow buntings may lay up to seven eggs with the average clutch size increasing with latitude. Most egg losses are due to nest predators; short-tailed weasels and Arctic foxes being the common culprits. The female incubates the eggs alone, and in most studied populations males fed their mate. The cold conditions in which the buntings nest probably encourages incubation feeding so that the female can remain on the nest and keep the eggs warm. After hatching, the chicks remain in the nest for roughly two weeks and then scatter, each parent caring separately for a portion of the clutch for an additional week or two. Afterward, juveniles quickly gather into flocks, some containing up to 100 individuals.

HOUSE SPARROW *Passer domesticus*

Family Details

Old World Sparrow Family (Passeridae), 40 species worldwide, 1 introduced prairie species

This is a small family of songbirds, most of whom live in Africa and India. All of them are seed-eating birds with short, conical bills adapted to crushing tough foods. One member of the family, the familiar house sparrow, was systematically introduced into North and South America, southern Africa, Australia, and New Zealand and has become one of the most successful avian colonists on Earth.

The story of the sparrow's introduction into North America is well known. In the spring of 1853, Nicholas Pike released a large number of these birds into Greenwood Cemetery in New York City. In the next two decades, other misguided bird lovers released the sparrows throughout New England, into the Midwest, into parts of eastern Canada, and into California, Texas, and Utah. In less than 100 years the bird colonized most of the continent—the fastest avian conquest ever recorded.

Field Identification

The male house sparrow is a small brownish bird with a gray cap, black bib, and white cheeks. The black bib is only present during the breeding season. The female sparrow looks the same year-round and is plain brown with a streaked back.

Where to Find

Although the house sparrow ranges throughout the continent from Arctic tundra to deserts and prairies, the bird occurs almost solely in association with humans and their buildings and is rarely seen elsewhere. In the prairies, large numbers of house sparrows live around grain elevators and farm buildings and are a common sight in every town and city.

Wintering Grounds

The tough little house sparrow winters on the prairies. The birds vary in size throughout the continent depending upon the climate; the largest sparrows live in the coldest climates. As a result, northern prairie house sparrows weigh more and have larger bodies than their relatives living farther south. The sparrows can endure temperatures colder than -20°C (-4°F), but to do so, they rely heavily on their fat reserves and a sheltered roost.

Diet and Feeding Habits

Looking at the stout conical beak of the house sparrow you could predict that the bird is a seed eater. Spilled grain, grass, and weeds seeds are its main diet. These birds, however, did not become as widespread as they are without a good measure of dietary flexibility. The adaptable house sparrow also eats beetles, grasshoppers, and weevils. They sometimes hunt flying insects attracted to lights at night, they will pierce flowers to steal the nectar, and I have often seen them scavenge dead insects from the front grill of my car.

Breeding Biology

The size of the black bib on the male house sparrow is a signal of rank; the larger the bib the higher the bird's rank and the greater his attractiveness to females. Since high-ranking males breed earlier and claim the best nest sites, why do male sparrows not simply cheat the system and grow larger bibs? The size of the bib is controlled by the male hormone, testosterone. In sparrows, high testosterone levels have a serious side effect; they suppress the bird's immune system, making them more prone to parasites and shortening their lifespan. Clearly, in house sparrows, the sexiest males pay a high price for their charisma.

High-ranking male sparrows commonly claim a nest site in autumn and control it all winter until the spring breeding season begins in April. House sparrows typically nest in cavities and choose the nooks and crannies in buildings and nest boxes. The sparrows are aggressive and will displace swallows, purple martins, and bluebirds from nest boxes, sometimes killing their rivals and building a nest over the bodies of the former owners. Typically, the birds build a domed nest of dried stems, feathers, string, and bits of cloth and paper. The female lays three to five greenish white eggs variably marked with dark spots and speckles. The monogamous pair share the two-week incubation of the eggs and take turns brooding the hatchlings until they are six days old and can keep themselves warm. Both parents feed the chicks regurgitated insects for the 14 days of nest life and for seven to ten days afterward. The independent youngsters join flocks of other juveniles that roost and forage together.

‹ These two male house sparrows have ›
different size bibs. Usually, the male
with the larger bib has a higher rank
and is more attractive to females,
and he generally breeds earlier and
occupies the best nest site.

WESTERN MEADOWLARK *Sturnella neglecta*

Family Details

Blackbird and Oriole Family (Icteridae), 98 New World species, 11 prairie species

This family of medium-sized songbirds contains many popular species including the western meadowlark whose fluid songs enliven the prairie landscape; the widespread red-winged blackbird, possibly the most abundant songbird in North America; and the resplendent orange-and-black Baltimore oriole—one of the most striking birds. For such a relatively small family, the blackbirds and orioles display a surprising variety of nesting habits. Some species cradle their eggs in pendulous nests high in the treetops, while others hide them on the ground. Many are solitary, but some cluster in dense colonies in cattail marshes. And while most members of this family tirelessly care for their eggs and chicks, some brown-headed cowbirds lay hundreds of eggs in their lifetime but never raise a single young. Instead, they lay their eggs in the nests of dozens of other birds and let the parasitized foster parents labor on their behalf.

Field Identification

The meadowlark is familiar to most prairie residents and hardly needs to be described. It is a medium-sized bird with bright yellow underparts emblazoned with a black V across its upper breast. The male and female are similar in appearance, although the female tends to be less brightly colored. In flight, the bird's white outer tail feathers are conspicuous and quite distinctive.

Where to Find

The western meadowlark is common and widespread in fields, pastures, and native grasslands throughout the prairies. The bird prefers open areas and rarely enters woodlands.

Wintering Grounds

In the central and southern prairies, the meadowlark is a year-round resident, but in the cold northern prairies, the birds migrate south into the United States and northern Mexico for the winter.

Diet and Feeding Habits

The meadowlark feeds mainly on the ground where it probes the soil with its wedge-shaped bill searching for fly larvae, ants, weevils, beetles, and cutworms. As well, it searches under clods of dried manure for crickets and dung beetles. The omnivorous meadowlark also eats grain, weed seeds, fruit, and occasionally preys on the eggs and young of other ground-nesting songbirds.

❮ *(top & left)* A territorial male meadowlark will move frequently around his territory, repeatedly broadcasting his defiant song to potential rivals in every direction. *(right)* This male has stuffed his beak with at least three army cutworm caterpillars (Noctuidae) plus a Jerusalem cricket (Stenopelmatidae) that he will feed to his ravenous chicks.

Breeding Biology

Adult males return to the prairies in April, two to four weeks before the females, and immediately begin their melodious dusk and dawn concerts from the tops of fence posts, wild rose bushes, and clumps of sagebrush. The bird's delightful flute-like bubbling song is the surest sign that spring has arrived on the prairies.

A territorial male may sing as many as six to nine different song types, attempting to outcompete his neighbors and lure a mate with an ear for quality. In a contest between neighboring songsters, a male may run through his entire repertoire, switching songs whenever his rivals do. Studies show that males with larger repertoires, which may signal the superior quality of the singer, attract a mate earlier and raise more young than do their vocally challenged competitors. Clearly, in the world of the meadowlark, the silver-tonged lover lures the most ladies.

The competition between rival males is not limited to vocal dueling. Veteran meadowlark researcher Dr. Wesley Lanyon wrote, "Body contact and fighting between males, though uncommon, can be quite severe with much thrashing of wings, jabbing of bills, and clawing. One combat lasted three minutes, during which the two males grappled so intently they tumbled awkwardly about on the ground."

More than half of male western meadowlarks entice two females to nest simultaneously in their territory, and a few males lure three. The birds nest on the ground, and although the nests are well concealed in thick grass, many are discovered by predators. Common "egg-nappers" and "chick-chompers" include skunks, coyotes, foxes, magpies, and crows. I learned firsthand about one of the more unusual predators. When I initially found the nest in question, it held four fuzz-covered chicks. I left it undisturbed and returned two days later to take a family portrait. When I parted the grass covering the brood, the nest was empty. I felt sick, and for an instant I blamed myself for the loss, believing my scent had attracted a predator. I parted the grass farther to examine the nest more closely, and there it was: a large prairie rattlesnake bulging from its most recent meal. The snake had eaten all of the nestlings. I took a quick mug shot of the culprit and then left it to digest its dinner in peace.

With so many predators scouring the prairie, it makes sense for meadowlark chicks to leave home as soon as they can, and the young fledge when they are just 10 to 12 days old. At this age, the youngsters have strong legs to run quickly and hide, but their flight feathers are not fully developed and they cannot fly. The young depend upon their parents to feed them for another two weeks while they grow and become independent.

→ **Trivia Tidbit**

The western meadowlark is the official state bird of Kansas, Montana, Nebraska, North Dakota, Oregon, and Wyoming, more states than any other bird.

RED-WINGED BLACKBIRD *Agelaius phoeniceus*

Family Details

Blackbird and Oriole Family (Icteridae), 98 New World species, 11 prairie species

See Western Meadowlark for a general discussion of the Blackbird and Oriole Family.

Field Identification

The male red-winged blackbird is unmistakable with his glossy black plumage and bright red shoulder patches. The female has a mottled brown back with heavy streaking on her undersides.

Where to Find

Red-wings are most common in cattail marshes, although they readily settle in hayfields, pastures, roadside ditches, and urban wetlands of every description.

Wintering Grounds

Red-winged blackbirds winter in the southern United States. Most leave the prairies rather late in the season, departing in October. The birds often settle in grain-producing areas, where they may mix with brown-headed cowbirds, starlings, and common grackles and form immense winter flocks, sometimes numbering several million birds. Red-wings return to the prairies in April.

⟨ A red-wing's usual clutch size is two to four eggs.

Diet and Feeding Habits

Red-wings typically forage on the ground by walking and probing the vegetation and the surface layers of the soil. For much of the year, the birds eat mostly seeds and grains, but on their prairie breeding grounds their tastes turn to animal foods, such as caterpillars, flies, spiders, aquatic beetles, and damselflies. One afternoon, I watched a brightly colored male red-wing feed his chicks lime-green caterpillars. The vibrancy and contrast of colors was hard to believe.

Breeding Biology

A male red-winged blackbird defends his territory with songs, aerial chases, and occasional grappling, wing-beating, bill-pecking battles. The bird's scarlet epaulets are important signals of dominance and ownership. When an inquisitive scientist blackened the red shoulder patches on a group of males, more than half of them immediately lost their territories to intruders. Red-wings are polygamous, and most males attract at least five female mates to their territory. Some "supermales" may lure up to 15 partners. A male has little hope of mating without a territory so competition is intense. A red-wing may live for 14 years, an exceptional lifespan for a songbird. A long life is advantageous since a male may wait years before it finally has a chance to

breed. Roughly 50 percent of males secure a territory by three years of age, but some may be five years old before they finally own some real estate.

A male red-wing's territory may be as large as half a football field, and it is a constant challenge for him to guard his partners from outside suitors. In fact, he almost always fails. DNA fingerprinting has shown that up to 48 percent of the offspring raised in a male's territory are fathered by another male, usually one of his neighbors.

Each female red-wing builds her own nest—a woven cup of decayed leaves, roots, and mud suspended between several cattail stalks, 20 to 80 centimeters (8 to 30 in.) above the water. In the 1930s, a patient biologist dissected a red-wing nest to see how it was made. The nest was composed of 142 strips of cattail leaves, 34 strips of willow bark, and 705 pieces of grass. Not surprisingly, the philandering males never help their mates with nest building or incubation. Even after the chicks hatch, some males never feed their offspring, but when they do help, the fledglings are heavier and more of them survive.

Young red-wings leave the nest after two weeks, and the parents feed them for up to five weeks afterward. Once they are independent, the youngsters join mixed flocks of juveniles and adults and forage and roost with the group until they migrate in the autumn.

‹ Both female (opposite) and male (left) red-wings use loud calls to attract a partner and intimidate rivals.

YELLOW-HEADED BLACKBIRD
Xanthocephalus xanthocephalus

Family Details
Blackbird and Oriole Family (Icteridae), 98 New World species, 11 prairie species

See Western Meadowlark for a general discussion of the Blackbird and Oriole Family.

Field Identification
The yellow-head is a medium-sized blackbird in which the male is nearly twice as heavy as the female. Males are glossy black with a striking orange-yellow head, neck, and breast. In flight, the handsome male displays conspicuous white wing patches. Female yellow-heads are an overall brownish color with a pale yellow chest and throat. The yellow chest and absence of prominent streaking in the female is the best way to distinguish her from the female red-wing with which she is sometimes confused.

Where to Find
The yellow-headed blackbird is found throughout the prairies in sloughs, ponds, and lakes wherever there are cattails and bulrushes growing in relatively deep water.

Wintering Grounds
Yellow-heads winter in the southern United States and Mexico. The bird is less tolerant of cold than the red-winged blackbird, and it migrates a month or so sooner, leaving the prairies in late August and early September. Its intolerance to cold also delays its spring return; most yellow-heads arrive back on the prairies in the early days of May.

Diet and Feeding Habits
The versatile yellow-head may forage in marshes, croplands, plowed fields, and native prairies. In wetland habitats, the bird

As the breeding season progresses a male ❯
blackbird's cleanly tipped wing and tail feathers
slowly become frayed and tattered from
rubbing repeatedly against coarse vegetation.

hops and climbs between the emergent stalks of vegetation gleaning aquatic invertebrates, such as dragonfly and damselfly nymphs, diving beetles, and spiders from the water surface and the plants. In drier habitats, it feeds on cutworms, army worms, ground beetles, fly larvae, caterpillars, weed seeds, and grains.

Breeding Biology

Male yellow-heads often group their territories together, so the birds appear to be somewhat colonial. Within a stretch of cattails or bulrushes, each male defends his own bit of turf, advertising his ownership with an elaborate display performed from an exposed perch. The rivals fan their tail, spread and droop their wings to expose the white patches, and point their beak skyward. Then, with all the gusto their hormone-charged bodies can muster they rattle and growl the most unmusical of calls.

In many sloughs and marshes, yellow-headed blackbirds often share the wetland with red-winged blackbirds. Both birds eat similar foods, so there is a potential for competition. As a result, yellow-heads, the larger of the two species, generally dominate red-wings, sometimes completely usurping the smaller birds' territories or relegating them to the margins of the marsh where the water is shallower. On the edges of prairie wetlands, there is a greater danger from mammalian predators,

This female had just begun to build a >
nest a half meter above the water in a
cluster of cattails.

such as skunks, mink, red foxes, and deer mice, which prey on many blackbird eggs and nestlings. Even with the protection of deeper water as many as 48 percent of yellow-head nests are destroyed by predators before the chicks fledge.

Yellow-heads are polygamous, and the most charismatic of males may lure up to eight females into his territory, although a harem of three or four is more typical. The females do most of the household duties. They build the nest, incubate the three to four eggs, and brood the chicks when they hatch as big-eyed, wrinkled blobs of life. After four or five days, the male yellow-head finally rises to the challenge of fatherhood and begins to help feed his offspring; although he pays most attention to the first of his mates and offers less help to the subordinate females in his harem.

When blackbird chicks first leave the nest at two weeks of age, they can only hop among the stalks of their cattail world. Within a week, they can flutter a meter or two (3 to 6 ft.) if needed, and by three weeks of age they can flap for 25 meters (82 ft.) or more. Chicks of this age often shadow their parents closely and noisily beg for food. The free lunches end soon afterward.

⟨ Several months after the start of the breeding season this male yellow-head is still singing his territorial song and illustrates the frayed tail feathers mentioned in the caption on page 226.

COMMON REDPOLL *Cardulelis flammea*

Family Details

Finch Family (Fringillidae), 168 species worldwide, 10 prairie species

The finches are a group of small to medium-sized, seed-cracking specialists. Although many different birds eat seeds some of the time, most switch to softer fruits and insects when they are available. Finches, on the other hand, eat seeds all of the time, and the shape of their beaks illustrates how well adapted these birds are to this type of food. Whereas blue jays and chickadees hammer seeds until they split, and grouse and mourning doves swallow them whole and grind them up in their muscular gizzards, most finches simply bite down hard with their powerful beaks until the seed cracks. The beak and jaws of a grosbeak, for example, are so strong that they can crush the hardest seeds, even cherry pits.

The finch family includes many species that normally live year-round in the boreal forest and the Arctic. The finches are hardy birds that can endure extreme cold if they have enough seeds to fuel their internal furnaces. When seed crops fail in the northern forests, as they do on a regular basis every two or three years, these birds have no option but to flee southward in winter to search for food. These periodic finch invasions, called irruptions, are eagerly awaited by prairie birdwatchers.

Field Identification

The common redpoll is a small, streaked, tan-and-white bird with a bright crimson forehead. In late winter, the male's breast is flushed with rosy pink as if it "had been dipped in strawberry juice." The birds commonly travel in flocks.

Where to Find

Flocks of these small beautiful finches may sometimes be flushed along roadsides in winter as they forage for weed seeds. However, they most often invade towns and cities where they cluster in birch trees and at bird feeders.

Wintering Grounds

The common redpoll, and its close relative the hoary redpoll, are winter visitors to the prairies. Weighing about 14 grams (0.5 oz.), the common redpoll is one of the smallest birds to overwinter. It survives the rigorous climate by tunneling at night into the snow where the temperature may be 22°C (40°F) warmer than the outside air. This resourceful little finch has another trick to get through the night. It chills out—literally. At night, a redpoll may let its body temperature drop by as much as 10°C (18°F), earning the bird a substantial energy saving.

The first flocks of redpolls arrive in the prairies from their Arctic breeding grounds in mid-October and disappear again by the end of March.

Diet and Feeding Habits

The redpoll eats the small seeds of many northern plants, including willows, alders, and poplars, but its favorite food is birch seeds. At the end of each winter day, the bird commonly stores extra food, particularly birch seeds, in a specialized pouch in its esophagus. During the night, when the redpoll is roosting, it can regurgitate the seeds if it needs extra energy. Researchers found that once a redpoll had filled up on birch seeds, it could survive a night when the temperature dropped to -62°C (-80°F). Without access to the calorie-rich seeds, however, the bird's limit was -30°C (-22°F).

Breeding Biology

The Arctic-nesting female redpoll builds a delicate cup nest of rootlets, grasses, and mosses, one to two meters (3 to 6.5 ft.) high in an alder or willow bush. The nest is often lined with ptarmigan feathers that insulate it against the predictable cold of a northern spring. The birds lay four or five beautiful pale blue eggs spotted with lilac and reddish brown scrawls and speckles. The drably colored female incubates the eggs alone, but both parents feed the young until they leave the nest at two weeks of age.

The common redpoll is a hardy winter ⟩
visitor to the prairies. Males *(far right)* and
females *(right)* travel together in mixed
flocks throughout the season and are
welcome visitors to backyard feeders.

PINE AND EVENING GROSBEAKS

Pinicola enucleator and Coccothraustes vespertinus

Family Details

Finch Family (Fringillidae), 168 species worldwide, 10 prairie species

See Common Redpoll for a general discussion of the Finch Family.

Field Identification

Both species of grosbeaks are plump, medium-sized birds with large conical bills. The male pine grosbeak has a dark red head, breast, back, and rump. The female has a gray body with a yellowish head and rump. The male evening grosbeak is easy to distinguish with its yellow body and dark brown head. The female evening grosbeak is grayish tan with a white-tipped tail, and a white patch on each wing.

Where to Find

The grosbeaks inhabit many prairie towns and cities during the winter months. They are among the most popular visitors at winter bird feeders.

Wintering Grounds

Both species of grosbeaks are strictly winter visitors. Usually, these beautiful birds arrive on the prairies in late autumn and leave in April or May to migrate north to their nesting grounds in the boreal forest. Grosbeaks are extremely gregarious and commonly travel in flocks of a dozen or two, and sometimes a group may number 100 birds or more. Pine and evening grosbeaks usually do not flock together, although they may gather at the same bird feeder.

Diet and Feeding Habits

In winter, these birds devour great numbers of sunflower seeds at bird feeders. Pine grosbeaks also feed on mountain ash berries, crab apples, and the seeds of spruce trees and Manitoba maples. Evening grosbeaks eat less fruit and concentrate more on the seeds of green ash, Manitoba maple, box elder, and paper birch. In spring, both birds eat the swelling buds of aspens and willows.

Breeding Biology

Both of these handsome seed crackers nest in the northern coniferous forests of the continent. The females of both grosbeaks build a loose cup nest of roots, twigs, mosses, and lichens high in a spruce or fir tree. Each lays a clutch of three to four eggs that are incubated entirely by the female while her faithful mate dutifully brings her meals of beetles, caterpillars, grasshoppers, flies, canker worms, and spruce bud worms. The same appetizing meals are fed to the hatchlings by both parents until the young leave the nest at roughly two weeks of age.

Both the pine grosbeak (here) and the ❯ evening grosbeak (next page) are regular winter visitors to the prairies and hold the distinction of having the strongest seed-cracking bills of any prairie bird.

ACKNOWLEDGMENTS

I still fondly recall my early friendships with photographers Fred Lahrman, Lorne Scott, and Gary Seib. It was 1977, my first summer on the prairies, and their enthusiasm for bird photography was infectious, and we shared many memorable outings. Ranchers Francis and Myrna Walker were also an important part of my early years on the prairies. They opened their home to me, and I will always remember their warmth and generosity.

In recent years, many local naturalists and skilled photographers were generous with their help and encouragement, including John Acorn, Carmen Avramovic, Dr. Robert Berdan, Dr. Gordon Court, Dr. Sharif Galal, Rob Hadlow, Ann Jones, Dave Lilly, Gerald Romanchuk, and Steve Schwartz. In the Brooks, Alberta, area I was assisted in my field endeavors by Daryl Burroughs as well as by Dan Buell, a biologist with the Eastern Irrigation District. I also want to thank photographer Ken Crebbin who generously invited me to photograph on his acreage and who provided me with one of his wonderful blue jay photos. I am especially indebted to professional photographer and raptor specialist Jon Groves who helped in many ways. Not only did he provide me with his superb photographs of a nesting pair of golden eagles and a western kingbird attacking a red-tailed hawk, he also taught me how to use a remote camera system and invited me on numerous field trips to photograph snowy owls, prairie falcons, and ferruginous hawks. I respect his field craft immensely and greatly value his friendship.

This is my 17th book with Fitzhenry & Whiteside, and I was so happy when Sharon Fitzhenry suggested we update and revise our 1999 book on prairie birds. Thank you, Sharon. It was a thrill to spend time on the prairies again. Special thanks to Chief Operating Officer Holly Doll, editor Charlene Dobmeier, and designer Tanya St. Amand for helping with this project. Hey, you folks, let's do this again.

Finally, I wish to thank my wonderful wife of 45 years, Aubrey Lang. Our countless adventures in the prairies are among my most treasured memories of our life together. Aubrey has been intimately involved in the planning and completion of every book I have ever written. She is an indefatigable field partner, an enjoyable campmate, and a skilled editor and advisor. I could not have done it without her.

‹ The author's wife, Aubrey Lang, enjoys a view of the meandering Milk River near the Montana/Alberta border.

ABOUT THE AUTHOR

In 1979, at the age of 31, Dr. Wayne Lynch left a career in emergency medicine to work full time as a science writer and photographer. Today, he is one of Canada's best-known and most widely published professional wildlife photographers. His photo credits include hundreds of magazine covers, thousands of calendar shots, and tens of thousands of images published in over 80 countries. He is also the author and photographer of over a dozen highly acclaimed natural history books for adults including *Windswept: A Passionate View of the Prairie Grasslands, Penguins of the World, Bears: Monarchs of the Northern Wilderness, A is for Arctic: Natural Wonders of a Polar World, Wild Birds Across the Prairies, Planet Arctic: Life at the Top of the World, The Great Northern Kingdom: Life in the Boreal Forest, Owls of the United States and Canada:* *A Complete Guide to their Biology and Behavior, Penguins: The World's Coolest Birds,* and *Galapagos: A Traveler's Introduction.* His books have been described as "a magical combination of words and images."

Dr. Lynch has observed and photographed wildlife in over 60 countries and is a Fellow of the internationally recognized Explorers Club, headquartered in New York City. A Fellow is someone who has actively participated in exploration or has substantially enlarged the scope of human knowledge through scientific achievements and published reports, books, and articles. In 1997, Dr. Lynch was elected as a Fellow to the Arctic Institute of North America in recognition of his contributions to the knowledge of polar and subpolar regions. And since 1996 his biography has been included in Canada's *Who's Who.*

‹ The author commonly uses a camouflaged blind to get intimate photographs of bird behavior with species that are sensitive and wary.